LESSONS
LEARNED FROM
EXPERIENCE:

A Practical
Developmental Source Book
For Educational Leaders

LESSONS
LEARNED FROM
EXPERIENCE:

A Practical
Developmental Source Book
For Educational Leaders

LARRY D. COBLE

ON TRACK PRESS, INC. · GREENSBORO, NORTH CAROLINA

On Track Press, Inc.
Greensboro, North Carolina

Cover and book designed by KCL Creative - Kerri Lindley, Ramseur, NC

Printed in the United States of America

ISBN: 0-9760355-0-2

Foreword

Larry Coble has written a very practical and pragmatic guide for helping existing school leaders develop their knowledge, skills, and dispositions toward administering effective school organizations, whether those organizations are at the school or district levels. Drawing from the experiences of practitioners and his own career as a teacher and school administrator, he has fashioned a powerful "do-list" for school leaders, things that can only make them better at what they do or hope to do. The lessons themselves almost emerge as a cross between a well-recognized leadership axiom and the sage advice from those who have indeed "been there and done that." Each lesson is divided into corollaries intended to help the learner focus on key elements of the lesson.

Dr. Coble posits twelve lessons in this book, lessons that speak to how one manages both the self and the organization so that both become better over time. Many of the lessons have familiar overtones, perhaps said in different ways. His first lesson speaks to the value of the school leader surrounding him or herself with passionate and competent people, a theme that Jim Collins articulated in his best-selling book, <u>Good to Great</u>. Coble goes several steps further and proposes specific activities school leaders can do to help ensure that condition in their organizations. His fifth lesson deals with the reality that not everyone may agree with you. His approach is to teach us to accept that as an inevitable, to seek ways to listen, and eventually to do what you, as leader, know is right. At the end of the day, the leader's moral compass should still be pointing to "true north." I particularly liked his corollary that pointed the leader to be an advocate for the powerless and voiceless in the school or school district. His point is these constituencies are as deserving of being "at the table" as anyone else, and the school leader can make sure that happens. The other lessons are equally compelling.

Several other characteristics of the book make it particularly appealing. First, all of the segments are short and pithy. No segment is longer than a page and a half, so the participant will likely not feel overwhelmed by voluminous narrative. Second, each lesson is accompanied by a self-assessment tool and some developmental templates to help guide continued growth and future action. The bridge between learning about leadership and doing leadership is inescapable. Third, after traversing the twelve lessons, Dr. Coble presents some case examples with analytic templates to enable the participant to apply the lessons in pretty authentic scenarios.

This book is very useful in settings where leadership development is needed, especially in settings where leaders may have lost either confidence or commitment to the power of their actions. Its appeal lies in its pragmatism and its readability. I would use this book both in leadership development workshops I might conduct and in courses for school leader "wannabees."

Kenneth D. Jenkins
Professor of Educational Leadership, Appalachian State University

CONTENTS

Preface

For nearly a decade, I have provided leadership training and development activities for thousands of school superintendents, district-level leaders, principals, assistant principals, and teacher leaders throughout the country. I also served as a teacher; assistant principal; principal; and, for over fourteen years, as a school superintendent. As a result of these experiences, I am convinced that one of the most productive developmental activities is to facilitate participants' learning by getting them to reflect upon their own experiences and the experiences of others who have faced similar challenges. This conclusion is based on feedback received from workshop participants, research that provides insight into how leaders develop, and my own experiences.

Approximately four hundred educational leaders from as many as fifteen states who have participated in our various leadership development projects were requested to record, in their own unique ways, leadership lessons that they had learned while carrying out their job responsibilities. The leaders came from small, large, rural, urban, and suburban settings. Some of their schools and districts were racially diverse and some were not. As a result, hundreds of statements were analyzed to determine whether a few basic leadership lessons could be logically derived because of the frequency in which they were mentioned and/or the compelling manner in which they were presented. The total number of recordings was initially sorted on the basis of content into twenty-one different lesson categories. Following additional reviews and analyses, the categories were reduced to the twelve basic lessons, along with the corollaries, that are included in this book.

This Source Book is designed to give practicing educational leaders and those who aspire to become leaders concrete, practical, and relevant ways to hone their leadership skills in their efforts to provide a better learning environment for students. Unlike many textbooks or articles on educational leadership, the lessons, principles and recommendations included in this publication were voiced and recorded by four hundred practitioners, who were at the time too busy from "fighting in the trenches," to devote time to publishing. In a way, the actual authors of this Source Book are those leaders who shared their wisdom and experience. This fact should make this publication more meaningful and helpful to readers, as practitioners continue to be our best teachers.

Larry D. Coble

Organization and Use

This Source Book includes twelve leadership lessons that were derived from my association with a large number of educational leaders who attended leadership training sessions sponsored by School Leadership Services. It also draws on my own experience of over twenty years as an educational leader in formal leadership roles. Each of the lessons contains a number of relevant principles, some cogent corollaries, and "pearls of wisdom" provided by the leaders. The Source Book is organized around each of the twelve lessons. It includes discussions, examples, suggested activities, ideas, and instruments for assessing the current status and change in behavior of the reader and action planning documents for developing on-the-job plans and activities. A suggested procedure for the reader to summarize what has been covered in the workbook and suggestions for applying the knowledge in the future are found at the end of the workbook. Note that space has been provided for you to record your own "pearls of wisdom." Finally, an opportunity to integrate the lessons is provided by way of cases/problems that capture real life leadership challenges for the reader.

The Source Book may be used in a variety of ways. For example, the book might serve as a user-friendly source book for obtaining ideas or inspiration for providing leadership training. The Source Book could also provide direction for conducting needs assessments and developing and implementing personal and group improvement plans. Perhaps the highest and best use is in a more structured way through the discussions, examples, activities, and assessments that will enable the reader to take charge of his or her own development. To facilitate your efforts to develop improvement plans, some simple planning procedures are presented at the end of this document.

The Twelve Lessons in the Source Book are:

Lesson 1. Competent Workers Are By Far The Most Important Assets In Determining Whether An Educational Leader And His/Her Organization Are Effective.

Lesson 2. Valid Information Is Essential In Making Wise Decisions, Developing Plans, And Evaluating Personnel And Outcomes.

Lesson 3. Strive To Be A Leader Among Leaders and A Leader Of Leaders.

Lesson 4. Leading Effectively Means Communicating Effectively.

Lesson 5. Accept The Fact That You Will Always Have To Contend With Opponents of Public Education.

Lesson 6. Although A Number Of School Leaders (Primarily Superintendents) Have Problems Working With Their Boards Of Education, School Boards Are One Of The Best Examples Of Democracy In Action And Can Be A Strong Asset In Operating The Schools.

Lesson 7. Your Job As A School Leader Is Important, But Keep Its Importance In Perspective – Your Life Is, Too!

Lesson 8. As A School Leader, You Cannot Be All Things To All People, Nor Can Schools Solve All Of Society's Problems.

Lesson 9. Keep In Mind That One Of The Most Effective Ways To Learn And Grow Is To Benefit From Your Critical Past Mistakes.

Lesson 10. Since Colleagues Are Probably Experiencing Or Have Experienced Difficulties Similar To Those You Are Now Facing, Networking And Using Mentors Are Effective Ways To Help Solve Problems.

Lesson 11. In Making Changes That Impact On The School Organization, Involve Representative Interested Parties In Analyzing Relevant Data And Developing Goals And Strategies. Disseminate Your Plans And Implementation Results To All Stakeholders.

Lesson 12. Remember, There Is One "Bottom Line" Criterion For Making Educational Decisions: What Effect Will The Decision Have On The Welfare Of Students?

Lesson 1

COMPETENT WORKERS ARE BY FAR THE MOST IMPORTANT ASSETS IN DETERMINING WHETHER AN EDUCATIONAL LEADER AND HIS/HER ORGANIZATION ARE EFFECTIVE.

- Employ the most competent people available.

- Exercise care in defining and delegating responsibility.

- Empower workers by letting them use their talents and providing them with resources and training.

- Appraise performance and hold employees accountable.

- Celebrate and reward exemplary work, and demote and discharge incompetent personnel.

UNDERSTANDING THE LESSON

Educational leaders feel that surrounding themselves with competent, energetic, and dedicated people not only makes the difference in their success as administrators, but also contributes to their own good mental health. The presence of competent employees affects their attitudes toward the nature of their work as the leaders are more motivated to complete the duties required of them in carrying out their job functions. When surrounding themselves with competent workers, the leaders believe that it is their responsibility to foster a climate that sets the tone for accomplishing school and district goals.

Helping others develop to their full potential is a priority for school principals. They provide professional growth opportunities through staff development and project assignments that allow for individual autonomy. The faculty and staff choose those activities that align with their unique abilities and individual needs. Many principals recognize and reward competent employees, on a regular basis, at a special time during faculty meetings, through "team player" certificates, restaurant and gift certificates, personal notes, e-mails, and other tokens that recognize outstanding performance and promote school spirit. These leaders cite that recognizing competence in this manner requires incredible energy, but the dividends of a loyal, visionary, and dedicated staff are the results of their efforts. An elementary principal said, "I see recognizing and developing leadership potential within the faculty as an important part of my job description. Further, recognizing the progress that each teacher leader makes toward her own development reinforces what we are all about in this school."

District-level leaders, including superintendents, are committed to surrounding themselves with competent employees and to empowering them to do their jobs. Many district-level leaders see hiring and empowerment as a central focus of top leadership. Senior leaders remove organizational barriers that cause people to feel helpless and then provide invitations for empowerment and success. A senior level leader in a large district office said, "Empowering others works best when you honestly believe that no one is more important than anyone else."

These district-level leaders encourage dissent through their request for honest feedback on their own performance. Honest feedback requires that senior leaders be candid with their colleagues and that they earn their trust by convincing their staffs that their actions are in the best interest of the larger organization and the specific group of people they are leading. If it appears that there are hidden agendas on the part of senior leadership, trust is replaced with alienation and a loss of effectiveness.

Surrounding yourself with competent workers requires that you build a team of honest, intelligent, and high-energy people. Then, you must provide direction and allow them to share in the successes of the organization. Sharing successes will cause them to renew their efforts and will generate even more success.

NOTES:

_____

_____

_____

_____

_____

_____

UNDERSTANDING THE COROLLARIES

Corollary 1
Educational leaders must be talent brokers. Building value congruence through the hiring process is critical. Effective leadership requires learning how to identify, recruit, and select future colleagues and how to work with those whose views differ from your own.

Practicing leaders subscribe to the ideal of seeking out the brightest and most competent people. They believe that their organizations will never reach their potential if quality people are not recruited. Once recruited, these talented individuals are expected to use their abilities to the fullest extent and are held accountable for their results.

Many leaders, particularly when implementing new initiatives or "start-ups," are given the opportunity to hand pick their staffs. A mid-career leader stated, "If you have had a little experience and have some idea of what you're doing, having an opportunity to pick and build your own staff can make the difference between success and failure."

Once selected, the leaders strive to build a trusting relationship with each team member, clearly communicate expectations, be honest, and be uncompromising in what they value in terms of organizational standards and individual performance. During faculty meetings at the school building level, many principals share the school's accomplishments to date, provide progress reports toward mission accomplishment, and keep the vision alive by constantly revisiting it with their faculties.

In brokering talent, effective leaders recognize the importance of seeking out candidates who, if employed, will bring a different perspective from that of the leader. They interview numerous people for a single position. They are also increasingly aware of the importance of other people's time and, as a routine practice, reschedule or cancel interviews only if it is absolutely necessary.

The ability to identify "raw" talent and then commit to the ongoing development of the individual hired is also characteristic of leaders at all levels of the organization. They trust their intuition about the potential leadership capacity of the candidates selected and commit to creating an environment of personal and professional development. In other words, effective leaders can recognize undeveloped talent; and, once they have made the hiring decision, move forward with the commitment to facilitate a learning environment that enhances growth and development.

NOTES:

_____

_____

_____

_____

_____

_____

_____

_____

_____

_____

_____

Corollary 2

Attitudes and motives make the difference. In addition to hiring the most competent people, make sure you employ individuals whose motives and attitudes are compatible with the school's mission and goals. There is no place in schools for individuals who do not have the best interest of students as their prime objective.

The leader who said, "I have grown to believe that attitude is just as important, if not more important, than aptitude," was referring to just how important positive attitudes and proper motivation are throughout the organization. District-level leaders, including superintendents, assess attitudes and motivation, as well as competence in assigning tasks. In so doing, they work at creating an environment of mutual respect and support, acknowledge the value of the skills that everyone brings to the job, celebrate successes along the way, and create and clearly communicate policies in a consistent manner.

When recruiting assistant principals, teachers, and other staff members, principals feel that most prospective employees are very conscientious and are properly motivated. During the interview process, the principals stress the organization's expectations and their personal expectations. As a result, many of those recruited, over the course of their careers, typically become upwardly mobile and move into a principalship or a central office position. Occasionally, the selection process will result in a less than satisfactory match. When there is not a good fit, many employees will choose to leave or to seek a better match somewhere else in the organization.

Leaders caution that it is sometimes necessary to terminate the employee when the match is poor and when the employee does not choose to leave on his/her own. Be prepared for the possibility that some who do not wish to leave will try to create conflict by contacting members of the board of education. The leaders tend to avoid serious repercussions, like having their decisions overturned, by keeping those who need to be informed "in the loop" along the way.

NOTES:

_____

_____

_____

_____

Corollary 3
Lost trust is seldom restored. Without the ability to establish and maintain trust, you will be unable to garner the support needed to lead effectively. To a leader, one's word is his/her bond.

Leaders at all levels throughout the school organization cite being honest and truthful, never compromising your basic values, not giving in to political pressure, being open, and admitting that you don't always have the answers creates an image of trustworthiness. School superintendents believe that they, and leaders at every level in the school district, must have a clear foundation of their purpose and values in their respective roles. What is important is often communicated by what you pay attention to and what you demonstrate that you respect through words and actions.

When leaders view someone as not being trustworthy, for whatever reason, they tend to write that person off. The superintendent of a small rural district said, "I don't have time to guess whether or not I can trust you. If you burn me once, I am not likely to place my confidence in you again."

Leaders attempt to forgive the act of untrustworthiness and move on, but they continue to remember the experience. Effective leaders learn from those they deem to be "snakes in the grass" and when they experience those who can't be trusted they realize just how difficult it can be to regain a reputation of trustworthiness. They are reminded of how important it is to establish and maintain trust themselves, if they are to lead effectively.

NOTES:

_____

_____

_____

_____

Corollary 4
Responding to great challenges is possible if you share the glory. When things are going well, give other's the credit. When things are not going well, accept the responsibility for the outcomes.

Leadership will be enhanced if you let those with whom you work know how much they are appreciated. Recognition by word-of-mouth, handwritten notes, formal celebrations, pay raises, promotions, contract extensions, and giving employees responsible jobs to perform demonstrate respect and appreciation. Through these acts of recognition, leaders send the message that staff is encouraged to take risks and innovate and the staff will be given credit for their successes. However, with risk-taking and innovation, not every outcome will be a successful one. In these situations, wise leaders accept the responsibility. Leaders know that if they punish failed risk-taking and innovative efforts, their staffs will freeze up and their schools, departments, and districts will not flourish.

Be on the lookout for people who aspire to greatness. Seek individuals who are ambitious, but not too ambitious. Specifically, look for those who might want your "position" some day, but avoid those who create an appearance that they will climb the organizational ladder at almost any cost. One leader with a reputation for identifying, recruiting, and developing outstanding talent said, "I look for those who are going to be high flyers, but who will remain with the flock." These are the people who will develop a plan for helping you achieve your goals and who will have the courage to see it through. Recognize their achievements and give them the credit. This will make your job easier.

NOTES:

_____

_____

_____

_____

Corollary 5
The successful educational leader develops familiar administrative structures, such as standing committees and well-understood problem-solving mechanisms, to move the organization toward desired goals. He/she is especially skillful at addressing new issues through existing familiar structures.

Successful educational leaders recognize that those persons whom they are charged to lead need to be able to understand and predict how things work in their organizations. Techniques used by leaders to ensure this familiarity and predictability include standing and called meetings, written agendas, the concept of leadership team, teachers' advisory council, students' advisory council, and the principals' association board of directors, just to mention a few. Standing committees of administrators and/or teachers, standard budget forms, familiar report formats, "blue ribbon" committees, the creation of ad hoc working teams to solve emergency problems, and other "habits" of organizations are among successful examples of familiar administrative structures. Structures, such as these, provide staff and community with much needed familiarity. These structures provide ways of handling routine issues, as well as mechanisms for addressing new issues when they arise. A suburban superintendent said, "Your employees want to be able to predict how you are going to behave as their leader. Familiarity with how things are done is something that is important to employees throughout the school district."

Developing standard ways of communicating with stakeholder groups like the school board, teachers' unions, and other publics are important. These stakeholders develop an expectation of how information will be "packaged" and received. When leaders vary from these standard ways of communicating, there are often resistance and claims of misunderstanding on the part of stakeholders.

Finally, it should be noted that having too many meetings, especially those that are nonessential, can be counterproductive. Finding a balance is very important.

NOTES:

_____

_____

_____

Corollary 6
Even the most competent workers must be involved in staff development activities to correct identified deficiencies and learn to carry out programs that are required to meet the needs of a changing world. The successful leader conducts regular assessments to identify strengths and developmental needs and then provides priority training.

One of the main jobs of an effective leader is to lead and manage continuous improvement within his or her organization. This is true whether you are at the district or building level. Leading continuous improvement means taking your school, your department, or your district and making it better over time. In order to do this, conduct on-going needs assessments and then align staff development with the most pressing needs of the organization. The key is to develop an understanding, through situational analyses/needs assessments, and then create a "tight" fit between what the organization needs to improve and the professional development designed to address the needs. Meaningful professional development that is focused and aligned with the needs revealed from a needs assessment and that is sustained over time is critical. A school principal who sees himself as consciously building the culture of his school said, "As accountability remains at the forefront, leaders must use professional development, along with nurturing and psychological support to help offset staff feelings of anxiety and incompetence."

NOTES:

_____

_____

_____

_____

ASSESSMENT INSTRUMENT TO DETERMINE THE EXTENT THAT YOU CURRENTLY EMPLOY OR HAVE IMPROVED IN THE USE OF EFFECTIVE PERSONNEL PRACTICES

Instructions: This instrument is designed to help you determine your current status and change in status relative to using effective personnel practices. Before reacting to the scale, decide whether you wish to appraise your current practices or the changes you have made in these practices over a particular period.

Current Status	*Rating*	*Change In Status*
Used to <u>very great</u> extent	5	Made <u>significant</u> positive change
Used to <u>great</u> extent	4	Made <u>some</u> positive change
Used to <u>moderate</u> extent	3	Made <u>little or no</u> change
Used to <u>a little</u> extent	2	Made <u>some</u> negative change
Used to <u>no</u> extent	1	Made <u>significant</u> negative change

Personnel Practices	Rating
1. Employs most competent available people.	5 4 3 2 1
2. Exercises care in defining and assigning responsibility.	5 4 3 2 1
3. Empowers workers by providing resources and training.	5 4 3 2 1
4. Appraises performance and holds workers accountable.	5 4 3 2 1
5. Celebrates and rewards exemplary work.	5 4 3 2 1
6. Demotes or discharges unproductive workers.	5 4 3 2 1
7. Develops and maintains trust and respect among employees.	5 4 3 2 1
8. Emphasizes the development of positive attitudes and motives.	5 4 3 2 1
9. Shares praise and glory of success with staff.	5 4 3 2 1
10. Develops effective administrative structures and procedures for attaining desired goals.	5 4 3 2 1
11. Provides staff development opportunities to correct deficiencies and carry out necessary change.	5 4 3 2 1
12. Uses procedures to make employees know that they work for a winning organization.	5 4 3 2 1

ON THE JOB DEVELOPMENT PLANS AND ACTIVITIES
(PERSONAL PRACTICES)

Instructions: The purpose of this chart is to provide you with a simple way for you to list your strengths and developmental needs, prioritize your improvement objectives, and list strategies that you might use to reach your goals. Reflect on past experiences and review all personal assessment data, including the previous page, to complete this task.

Strengths	Developmental Needs

Improvement Objectives	Possible Strategies

"BACK HOME" APPLICATIONS
(Personnel Practices)

Instructions: Based on your understanding of the lesson and the corollaries, pick one or two of the skills and consider your previous experiences and possible future applications "back home" in your leadership role.

SKILL	*PREVIOUS EXPERIENCE*	*FUTURE APPLICATIONS*
Employ Competent Workers,		
Talent Brokering,		
Compatible Motives and Attitudes,		
Establishing Trust,		
Sharing the Glory,		
Developing Familiar Administrative Structures, and		
Prioritizing Staff Development		

Lesson 2

VALID INFORMATION IS ESSENTIAL IN MAKING WISE DECISIONS, DEVELOPING PLANS, AND EVALUATING PERSONNEL AND OUTCOMES.

- Create and maintain a comprehensive database about all major education functions.

- Use the "best" available information in making decisions and implementing major change initiatives.

- Disseminate information to promote education, demonstrate needs and challenges, and to celebrate the successes of employees and programs.

UNDERSTANDING THE LESSON

Consensus among educational leaders in today's climate of high-stakes testing and greater accountability is that it is important to make decisions that are data driven and based on accurate information. However, in making data-driven decisions, it is important to develop the ability to make very complex information easily understandable. There are no shortcuts to doing your "homework" as an educational leader. It is imperative that leaders understand the "why" behind what has to be done and then communicate this information to employees in terms that they can understand.

The abundance of information so readily available requires that leaders develop the skills to decipher the information and select that which is relevant and most useful for the task at hand. In addition to the sheer amount of information available to educational leaders, the nature of bureaucracies is such that rumors, gossip, and an irresistible movement of paper serve as barriers to getting the "best" available information.

Superintendents note that it is important to keep in mind one's audience when sharing information or attempting to secure information. These leaders adapt their approaches and communication styles, based on the uniqueness of each situation. At times, the circumstances may call for a more formal approach; at other times, an informal exchange will occur, depending on the purpose and setting. A superintendent in a mid-west community said, "Over the years I've worked hard at learning to read my audience. I am not batting a hundred percent, but most of the time I can read their body language and I've done my homework in order that I might gauge what to expect."

Superintendents further state the importance of a system-level public information officer who is skilled at directing the flow of positive information and who is proactive in doing so. Embedded in the responsibilities of the public information officer is the requirement that the officer can handle the press and other media in a crisis situation. In general, educational leaders should retain a calm, reassuring demeanor when seeking the "best"information available and whether they are sharing positive or negative "news."

Regarding the board of education, superintendents believe that it is important to keep the board informed of the kind of data that are being used to drive decision making, share general information viewed to be of importance to the board, and provide meeting agendas well in advance of regular and called board meetings. Above all, there should be no "surprises" for the board. The superintendent is ultimately the "teacher of the organization," whether communicating with the general community, special interest groups, the board of education, or district or building-level staff.

Building-level leaders, when facing highly complex decision-making processes like implementing federal guidelines for special programs, find that teachers tend to feel overwhelmed. In order to offset teacher confusion and frustration, these principals break the process down into rational and simplified steps, thereby turning what appears to be an unmanageable situation into a logical, sequential, and more manageable approach to decision making. An elementary principal stated, "I certainly don't ever try to hide things from my faculty, but instead I protect them. In other words, I tell them what they need to know when they need to know it and avoid information overload."

Many educational leaders, at all levels, struggle with whether or not they are making the best decision. To enhance the probability of making more effective decisions, these leaders review data, reflect, and talk with others before coming to a final decision. The wisest of leaders recognize how much they need the input of others. They explore other's thoughts, ideas, and advice. A deputy superintendent in a large district said, "There is so much on my plate that it helps me to think out loud with trusted colleagues." This is affirming and for some leaders this style requires more patience than they would normally exercise. Yet, they feel more fulfilled and are happier with their efforts.

Finally, sharing information with stakeholders, inviting feedback, and empowering them to share in the decision-making process avoids the pitfall of limited participation and misunderstanding. Examples include such approaches as revisiting and rewriting mission statements and school improvement plans, sharing and discussing detailed test data, discussing the implications of socio-economic status of students, planning staff development, assessing the computer competency level of students, developing goals for the use of technologies in classrooms, and budget development.

NOTES:

_____

_____

_____

_____

_____

_____

_____

_____

_____

_____

_____

UNDERSTANDING THE COROLLARIES

Corollary 1
Data obtained with the implementation of the new state and federal accountability programs (high-stakes testing) provide school personnel with invaluable information for developing strategies to improve students' academic performance and the quality of instruction.

Test data that are disaggregated by such variables as gender, race, and educational levels of students' parents provide clues about student performance and what can be done to improve student performance. Test reports that provide instructional objectives and item scores open up excellent opportunities for providing prescriptive and remedial instruction. One of the first major steps, which must be taken by schools to meet accountability standards and improve instruction, is to assure that there is an excellent alignment between the written, taught, and tested curricula.

In today's environment, some leaders utilize a "data" team to analyze small portions of relevant data applicable to a specific concern or challenge. Examples include such issues as analyzing student attendance data as a means of evaluating an out-of-school suspension policy, helping parents understand subject choices for students, and rewriting the teacher handbook in order to make it more user friendly. Graphic representations are used to make some forms of data more understandable. The benefits of using a team approach are outlined by a principal who believes, "If I bring those most affected all the way into the data analysis process, I can expect an extraordinary amount of support when the data are analyzed and when it's time to go to work."

NOTES:

_____

_____

_____

_____

Corollary 2
The development and timely use of customized needs assessment instruments is an effective technique for identifying the strengths and developmental needs of the schools.

Needs assessment instruments are a valuable leadership tool and can be made user friendly. They are especially useful in identifying problems or needs that might be addressed in developing comprehensive school improvement plans. Some leaders facilitate the development of needs assessment instruments by having their staffs participate in the development process. The needs assessment serves as a kind of research effort that allows for documentation in advance of introducing a change project. Further, in anticipation of changes that might come about as a result of utilizing a needs assessment, many effective leaders keep a current file on promising research practices that can promote change initiatives. An assistant superintendent who has a major responsibility with accreditation activities acknowledged, "I've found that, if I keep a file on best practices, I can share these at staff meetings and we are all then at a kind of level playing field."

NOTES:

_____

_____

_____

_____

Corollary 3
The enterprising educational leader develops a system for identifying, retrieving, and storing information about exemplary programs that can readily be adopted or adapted to improve his/her school/system.

Administrators, teachers, and support staff are encouraged to identify and field test promising approaches that might lead to improved practices in the school or district.
In order to plan for innovations, leaders encourage the development and value the use of conceptual skills throughout their organizations. Innovations that are well-conceived and planned are given an opportunity whether they work out or not.

Enterprising educational leaders, as they climb the ladder of leadership, face increasing scrutiny. Their supporters and critics judge practically every major decision and almost every statement that they make. Superintendents especially feel that, rightly or wrongly, their every action is evaluated by "armchair quarterbacks." A late career superintendent said, "It doesn't matter what I decide. Half the people will be happy with my decision and the other half will not. Those who are displeased think that they have all the answers."

The leaders suggest that one's effectiveness can be enhanced by calling on past experiences, simplifying what is being proposed, and storing information that can be retrieved later to solve future problems. Experience counts for so much. Just be careful in jumping to conclusions in an attempt to reach closure too quickly.

NOTES:

_____

_____

_____

_____

Corollary 4
The successful educational leader communicates effectively and creates order and promotes cooperation by simplifying interpretations and providing rationales for the existence of problems or the solutions to issues.

District and building-level leaders alike find that the nature and complexity of what needs to be communicated within their organizations cannot be done so effectively unless the information is simplified. Public bureaucracies tend to stifle effective communication in one way or another. A central office veteran cautions, "We have to be careful that we don't spend all of our time serving the bureaucracy rather than having the bureaucracy serve us." Leaders admit to the fact that they must learn more about how bureaucracies operate. To assist them in navigating the "murky" waters, many leaders strive to get feedback on how they are perceived as leaders; they observe more and take notes; and they keep personal journals in order to spend more time in reflection.

It is commonly recognized that the use of language and general communication skills, both verbal and non-verbal, can be the most powerful skills that a leader can possess. Most effective leaders believe that unless you are an effective communicator, possession of all the other leadership attributes that would make one successful will not guarantee success. A high school principal in the west said, "Don't forget, you're always communicating; and it's either positive or negative in the minds of the listeners."

Often, leaders will "mingle" with their staffs in an informal manner to try and connect with them in ways that make communication easier. In a more formal approach, some leaders say that they put everything of any magnitude in writing. Due to the fact that leaders are always "on stage" and those in their presence tend to do selective listening, it is extremely helpful to have the "listener" state back to you what you said, as well as the interpretation of what was said. This technique tends to minimize the distortion between what was said and what was heard, since the listener controls what is heard.

When it comes to communicating with the media, some leaders admit that their views have been skewed due to negative relationships with a few reporters in the past. This frequently means overcoming an attitude that one "should not trust any reporter." Leaders see media representatives as individuals with agendas to gather news, either positive or negative, with more of a slant toward the negative, but not as individuals who wish to accommodate the school organization. It is possible, however, to have a positive working relationship with the media and it begins by treating each media representative as a colleague. It is frequently helpful to provide an "official" response to newsworthy events. One local administrator said, " I can't remember who said it, but it sure is true—never pick a fight with anyone who buys their ink by the barrel."

There is often a discontinuity between the way individuals talk about issues in private and the way they talk about them in public. Meetings of school boards often demonstrate this idea as issues with many strained aspects are presented and discussed with a smoothness that belies the truth. The superintendent of a metropolitan school district said, "I have a few board members who literally despise each other; but, when they get in front of the cameras at our televised board meetings, butter will melt in their mouths." It is often helpful to cut through jargon that is confusing, strive to communicate in a fashion that reduces friction over highly charged issues, and present clear and concise messages.

NOTES:

_____

_____

_____

_____

ASSESSMENT INSTRUMENT TO DETERMINE THE EXTENT THAT CURRENTLY EMPLOY OR HAVE IMPROVED IN THE EFFECTIVE USE OF VALID INFORMATION

Instructions: This instrument is designed to help you determine your current status and change in status relative to effectively using valid information. Before reacting to the scale, decide whether you wish to appraise your current practices or the changes you have made in these practices over a particular period.

Current Status	*Rating*	*Change In Status*
Used to <u>very great</u> extent	5	Made <u>significant</u> positive change
Used to <u>great</u> extent	4	Made <u>some</u> positive change
Used to <u>moderate</u> extent	3	Made <u>little or no</u> change
Used to <u>a little</u> extent	2	Made <u>some</u> negative change
Used to <u>no</u> extent	1	Made <u>significant</u> negative change

Use of Valid Information	Rating				
1. Develops and maintains comprehensive system for collecting and retrieving valid instructional and management information.	5	4	3	2	1
2. Summarizes and disseminates relevant information to staff and other education stakeholders.	5	4	3	2	1
3. Trains personnel to collect, retrieve, analyze, and use information.	5	4	3	2	1
4. Disaggregates test data to assist in instructional decisions and planning.	5	4	3	2	1
5. Collects and disseminates information about exemplary instructional and management programs.	5	4	3	2	1
6. Conducts timely and meaningful needs assessments.	5	4	3	2	1
7. Uses all types of information for developing long-range plans.	5	4	3	2	1
8. Uses valid information to conduct personnel performance appraisals.	5	4	3	2	1
9. Provides members of school board with relevant information about items that will be discussed at next board meeting.	5	4	3	2	1
10. Provides adequate technology and equipment to collect and analyze data.	5	4	3	2	1
11. Establishes policies and procedures to assure privacy rights.	5	4	3	2	1
12. Assures the proper alignment between curriculum requirements and instruction and disseminates this information.	5	4	3	2	1

ON THE JOB DEVELOPMENT PLANS AND ACTIVITIES
(USE OF VALID INFORMATION)

Instructions: The purpose of this chart is to provide you with a simple way for you to list your strengths and developmental needs, prioritize your improvement objectives, and list strategies that you might use to reach your goals. Reflect on past experiences and review all personal assessment data, including the previous page, to complete this task.

Strengths	Developmental Needs
Improvement Objectives	**Possible Strategies**

"BACK HOME" APPLICATIONS
(Use of Valid Information)

Instructions: Based on your understanding of the lesson and the corollaries, pick one or two of the skills and consider your previous experiences and possible future applications "back home" in your leadership role.

SKILL	*PREVIOUS EXPERIENCE*	*FUTURE APPLICATIONS*
Valid Information in Decision Making, **Data Based on State/Federal Accountability,** **Needs Assessments,** **Identifying, Storing, and Retrieving Information, and** **Communicating Effectively**		

Lesson 3

STRIVE TO BE A LEADER AMONG LEADERS AND A LEADER OF LEADERS

- Convey to each and every employee that he/she is a "unit president" or the main "leader" in the unique job to which he/she is assigned.

- Make yourself accessible to workers who have legitimate reasons to confer with you. Get in the trenches with employees. Let employees know who you are as a person outside of your official leadership role.

- Delegate responsibility to staff members who are more competent in doing a job than you.

- Provide leadership training across the system, not just for top and middle management.

UNDERSTANDING THE LESSON

When leaders create conditions for others to feel that they are important, they begin to develop a system of loyal employees who will do what they need to do to help the school or district be successful. Those under your supervision will respond based on your words and actions. Demonstrate your intent through a model of servant leadership and visible actions that you are willing to do even the mundane tasks. One highly effective leader said it this way, "I don't mind taking my coat off, rolling up my sleeves, and getting my hands dirty. I never ask anyone to do anything that I wouldn't be willing to do myself."

Make a concerted effort to let everyone know that they are a valuable part of the team. When you take the lead in modeling this behavior, others will be inclined to follow. If your staff is, in your mind, irreplaceable, then let them know it.

Leaders maintain visibility with their staffs by constantly being seen on their campuses or throughout their offices. They walk around the grounds; they visit classrooms; they monitor student behavior in the cafeteria; and they are always on the lookout for positives, seeking situations that allow them to communicate the worthiness of others. Be a leader who is accessible to those you are leading. A summarizing quote from a building-level administrator expressed her sentiments this way, "With all the demands that are placed on school leaders, I sometimes have to make myself step out of my office and get into the classrooms and hallways. That face-to-face contact, although for brief intervals, makes all the difference in how I am perceived."

25

In striving to be a leader among leaders, practitioners identify staff members with the highest potential for leading and assign responsibilities that ensure early successes. A superintendent said, "The problems facing schools today are too great for a handful of leaders to go it alone. We must develop the leadership capacity in everyone and at every level. I am always on the lookout for those who want to share in the leadership responsibilities." Effective leaders provide leadership training for their entire staffs. Upon returning from professional development activities, they feel a responsibility for reporting their experiences and learning to their staffs.

NOTES:

_____

_____

_____

_____

UNDERSTANDING THE COROLLARIES

Corollary 1
Effective collaborative partnerships require being supportive of one's partners. Being aware of the needs of all partners, including those who can't do something for you, like your lowest paid employees, yields positive dividends.

If you are a district-level leader, you must avoid a division between your staff and those in the schools. If you are leading a school, you must avoid a division between your staff and the district office. Experience teaches leaders at all levels that nothing positive will come from alienating those who have a stake in the outcomes that your school or district is trying to produce. We must no longer tolerate, at any level, an "us versus them" mindset. A principal of a high-performing school said, "We're all in this together, and I will not tolerate finger pointing. When you are on a team, you all pull for each other."

Strive to involve all stakeholders whenever you can, and build partnerships at every opportunity. Plan and participate in retreat activities that involve both district staff and building-level staff. District administrators must visit schools on a regular basis, mingle with teachers, and make a strong effort to understand what is happening at the building level. When district staff visits schools, the school-based personnel gain a confidence in the central administration and this in turn builds much needed credibility.

As a building-level administrator, enhance your partnership with teachers by visiting classrooms. Personally cover classes for teachers who have doctors' appointments and other personal needs to be away from school, become more hands-on, and learn more about the instructional program. If a cafeteria worker becomes ill, take your turn in the serving line. If custodians need help cleaning or unloading furniture, assist when you can. Foster the development of partnerships through an attitude of inclusion. Arrange social events that include all personnel. One high school principal said, "In our school, we have found that the true team building occurs when we are playing together. Some how, just being away from the day-to-day stresses for a little while causes us to appreciate one another's humanity a little more."

Build partnerships with parents by collaborating on student recognition programs, curriculum, and athletic and other extracurricular issues. Take the time to speak to community groups about local concerns, as well as about state and national issues. Work with your business community in identifying ways that they can support your school.

NOTES:

_____

_____

_____

_____

_____

_____

_____

_____

_____

Corollary 2
If you really want to be a leader of leaders, you must set a good example. Asking followers to abide by the old "axiom" which says "do as I say, not as I do" won't work. An effective leader fully realizes that no one is always perfect and admitting mistakes goes a long way in establishing credibility.

Leaders who fail to recognize that they do not have all the answers are doomed to fail. A distinguishing characteristic that differentiates highly successful leaders from those who are less successful is that those who are successful see the admission of a mistake as a strength as opposed to a weakness. In today's highly stressful environment, however, all leaders are subject to take on too much personal responsibility. In this context and under the mandates of accountability, many leaders have to work overtime to address the relationship aspects of their jobs. Their task orientation to get the job done is so strong that they must constantly remind themselves to make time to be social and attend to the relationship needs of their colleagues. So, recognize the importance of each person under your direction and see each one not only as a colleague, but also as a potential friend.

A visible example of not having all the answers is delegating and then avoiding micromanaging. Superintendents note that, when there is a pattern of a large volume of turnover in personnel, they tend to delegate less. At the same time, they recognize the need to set parameters for their staffs and then hold them accountable. Principals say that they want to delegate responsibility and be visible, but feel that they are pulled in so many different directions that they have become reactionary. In an effort to support their staffs, principals, strive to maintain constancy, accessibility, and create supportive structures, but they report it takes a toll on them. Leaders who try to be everything to everybody get into trouble. A highly respected senior-level leader said it this way, "For many years, I tried to be everything to everybody, and I was about to burn out. Through some serious soul searching, I learned how to find high leverage activities that allowed me to accomplish just as much or more with less effort. We have worn it out, but I guess I learned how to work smarter."

One way of controlling your accessibility and, at the same time, not alienating your staff is to use a modified open door policy when someone wishes to meet with you in your office. This is true at any level in the organization. Basically, you agree to see anyone who wishes to meet with you; but, unless it is an absolute emergency, they must get on your calendar. This idea is easier to implement at the central office as a superintendent or district-level leader than at the building level. However, it does hold promise for reducing reactionary responses. Also, when leaders are visible outside of their offices, it creates opportunities for informal conversations with those who might otherwise request a formal meeting.

Model visibility at public events and create positive interactions with members of the school community. Take advantage of these types of settings to promote your school and district. Publicly praise your teachers and share the beliefs that are a foundation for the work that is done in the schools and the district. A wise superintendent said, "You must recognize that, as the formal leader, you are expected to be visible. At the same time, most of your constituents are going to judge your schools on what goes on in the classroom between their child and their child's teacher. Be visible and always speak highly of the job your teachers are doing."

Leaders who are driven to high achievement must work at attaining more life balance, seeking to be better rounded. Although extremely difficult, leaders must visibly demonstrate an expectation that those that they lead have a life outside of work. Learn through behavioral changes that it is important for you and those you lead to plan time for socialization and renewal activities.

NOTES:

_____

_____

_____

_____

Corollary 3
Confidence in yourself and your employees is critical for success. Believing in yourself, as well as those who work with and for you, is the foundation upon which progress is realized.

Set the example of being a confident leader. To succeed in school administration, having a thick skin is a prerequisite for the job. Being confident in yourself and having confidence in those whom you lead will serve you well. Confidence requires a strong ego. A strong ego is considered a strength for leaders. Be confident, but not arrogant. Balance your leadership approach with both support and pressure. Know when to give your staff a pat on the back and know when to take a tougher approach. One leader said, "To be effective, you must know when to care and when to use tough love."

Believe in yourself and your organization, focus on your mission, and use your belief system as a basis for confidence in yourself and your employees. A confidence builder is to remind all stakeholders, both within the school or district and external to the school or district, of the positive happenings throughout the organization. Leaders believe that, when they emphasize good news, we all feel better about our organizations and ourselves.

Superintendents and other district-level leaders summarize positive facts about their districts and share these with faculties, Parent Teacher Associations, and when making speeches throughout the community. Some leaders write weekly editorials to share information about local, state, and national educational affairs. Others use newsletters and communicate regularly with the media. An unusual and interesting confidence builder is to accept an invitation to speak on a subject that you know little about, do the research, and learn as much about the topic as you can in preparation for your presentation.

NOTE:

_____

_____

_____

_____

Corollary 4
One measure of a leader is his/her willingness to learn from those who report to him/her; you can't be an expert in everything.

There is a great advantage to turning every leadership challenge into a learning laboratory. Some of your greatest lessons will involve learning from others. This includes learning from others' successes, but most of all from their mistakes. Utilize mentors and always maintain a posture of being humble. Young administrators, in particular, can learn from almost everyone with whom they come in contact. One leader stated, "I learned more from my custodian than from all of my leadership classes."

When learning from others, give them your full attention. Don't make the mistake of halfway listening. Work at blocking out thoughts that are getting in the way of your hearing what is being said. Try to focus on whether or not there is a hidden message behind the words that might be conveyed by body language and speech patterns. Analyze not only the words, but the actions of others.

NOTES:

_____

_____

_____

_____

Corollary 5
One of the best ways to become a leader is to know the difference between being a leader and a position holder.

A leader is certain that success is based on ability and hard work. Position holders who are unsuccessful claim that work is unduly influenced by circumstances over which they have no control. A leader accepts that luck has a bearing on achievement, but is convinced that one can affect luck. Position holders believe that chance plays a major role in what is accomplished. Leaders have a love for work. Position holders show little enthusiasm for work. Leaders are endowed with vigor and energy. Position holders lack energy and are passive. Leaders are considered by most to be a "winner." Position holders are viewed in less than high esteem. An entry-level administrator said, "Leadership is about a person and a process, not a position."

NOTES:

_____

_____

_____

_____

**ASSESSMENT INSTRUMENT TO DETERMINE THE EXTENT THAT
YOU ARE CURRENTLY STRIVING OR HAVE CHANGED IN THE
EXTENT YOU STRIVE TO BE A LEADER AMONG LEADERS
AND A LEADER OF LEADERS**

Instructions: This instrument is designed to help you determine your current status and change in status relative to being a leader among leaders and a leader of leaders. Before reacting to the scale, decide whether you wish to appraise your current practices or the changes you have made in these practices over a particular period.

Current Status	*Rating*	*Change In Status*
Used to <u>very great</u> extent	5	Made <u>significant</u> positive change
Used to <u>great</u> extent	4	Made <u>some</u> positive change
Used to <u>moderate</u> extent	3	Made <u>little or no</u> change
Used to <u>a little</u> extent	2	Made <u>some</u> negative change
Used to <u>no</u> extent	1	Made <u>significant</u> negative change

	Indicators of Striving to Be Leader of Leaders	**Rating**
1.	Conveys to each staff member that he/she is a key leader in his /her unique job.	5 4 3 2 1
2.	Delegates responsibilities to competent staff members.	5 4 3 2 1
3.	Makes self accessible to staff who need to confer.	5 4 3 2 1
4.	Provides leadership training to all, not just top and middle management.	5 4 3 2 1
5.	Takes time to socialize with staff and board members when away from the job.	5 4 3 2 1
6.	Maintains visibility in community.	5 4 3 2 1
7.	Sets a good example for staff.	5 4 3 2 1
8.	Understands differences between leader and "loser" behavior.	5 4 3 2 1
9.	Believes in self and staff.	5 4 3 2 1
10.	Admits mistakes.	5 4 3 2 1
11.	Continues to work after experiencing setback(s).	5 4 3 2 1
12.	Uses compassion and "tough love" effectively.	5 4 3 2 1

ON THE JOB DEVELOPMENT PLANS AND ACTIVITIES
(STRIVING TO BE A LEADER AMONG LEADERS
AND A LEADER OF LEADERS)

Instructions: The purpose of this chart is to provide you with a simple way for you to list your strengths and developmental needs, prioritize your improvement objectives, and list strategies that you might use to reach your goals. Reflect on past experiences and review all personal assessment data, including the previous page, to complete this task.

Strengths	Developmental Needs

Improvement Objectives	Possible Strategies

"BACK HOME" APPLICATIONS
(Striving to Be a Leader Among Leaders and a Leader of Leaders)

Instructions: Based on your understanding of the lesson and the corollaries, pick one or two of the skills and consider your previous experiences and possible future applications "back home" in your leadership role.

SKILL	*PREVIOUS EXPERIENCE*	*FUTURE APPLICATIONS*
Leader Among Leaders,		
Setting a Good Example,		
Being Confident,		
Willingness to Learn from Others, and		
Leading Versus Holding a Position		

Lesson 4

LEADING EFFECTIVELY MEANS COMMUNICATING EFFECTIVELY.

- Keep all key stakeholders (board, staff, students, media, and others) informed of the happenings, both good and bad, in the schools.

- Return phone calls and answer letters in a prompt manner.

- Make a major effort to inform all interested parties of the role education plays in making America strong intellectually and economically.

- Refrain from communicating false or inaccurate information.

- Remember that communication is a two-way street; listening is just as important as talking.

UNDERSTANDING THE LESSON

Superintendents, along with other district-level leaders, recognize the importance of communicating one's goals, mission, and beliefs clearly. It is important to refrain from overwhelming the listeners by keeping your ideas simple and getting them to engage in thinking about how what you are saying has application to their needs and wants. It is sometimes important to construct "trails of information" for the purpose of generating feedback before a directive or mandate is given

When attempting to attack the sacred cows in the organization, do so in a way that keeps you removed from the direct hit if possible. Use outside groups and consultants to assist with projects that will tarnish you to the point that you will be rendered seriously ineffective. In discussing an outside group that was brought into his district to conduct a curriculum audit, one superintendent stated:

> I found the public sentiment so strong for maintaining the tracking system in our schools that, if I had attacked it directly early on, I would have been run out of town. However, by using an outside group to tell the same thing that I would have said, some of the fallout was minimized. My board and the community didn't like hearing what the outside group said, but the process resulted in the elimination of unfair tracking practices; and I kept my job.

Seek input through informal means such as chatting and visiting with various stakeholder groups. Invite them to share their perceptions with you. Seek feedback on what's working well in the organization and what is not before making changes. Read the environment and assess your stakeholders and their needs.

Most leaders recognize that communication is the key to having a successful organization and that it is necessary to have a number of ways for sending and receiving information. The use of feelers or "bread crumb trails" is a method frequently used. By leaking information, leaders are able to see who will respond and in what ways. This creates an arena in which the unique insights of those who may be affected by the decision have an opportunity to react before plans and decisions are finalized. A senior leader pointed out the fact that some people do not agree with her approach, but she said, "I find it extremely beneficial, especially with controversial decisions, to leak information in front of the final decision and see what kind of reaction I get."

Developing leaders realize that they can never become too skilled at communicating. Working on one's ability to communicate orally, articulating one's vision for the school or district, and working with other educational leaders to help solve common problems are effective leadership strategies. Upon moving from a rural superintendency to a higher profile small city district, one superintendent said:

> My board supported me, but they were open in telling me that I needed to be a little more polished with my increased visibility with a more sophisticated public. So they asked if I would mind working with a public relations firm on my image. At first, I was offended, but went ahead. It turned out to be one of the best things I have ever done to address my own development.

NOTES:

_____

_____

_____

_____

UNDERSTANDING THE COROLLARIES

Corollary 1
Communication is the single most powerful leadership tool. Without the ability to communicate effectively, the most talented educational leader will fail.

Informing teachers and staff about pertinent issues and important events is how many building-level leaders spend much of their time. The goal is to involve the staff in developing a comprehensive understanding of the issue that is at hand. In the process, efforts should be made to make certain that all who wish to express an opinion have an opportunity to do so. Opinions, once heard, are valued. This communication effort allows for the establishment of clear expectations for faculty and staff and involves them directly in the process. One middle school principal said, "I learned the hard way the problem of too limited participation."

Principals, assistant principals, and, to some extent, district-level leaders use contacts with parents as a way of keeping informed about what is currently buzzing or being rumored in the community. Scheduling regular or standing meetings of advisory groups is also helpful. Make certain that the advisory groups visibly demonstrate that diversity in membership is valued. Basic methods for keeping parents and other stakeholder groups informed of school events are newsletters, automated telephone calling systems, and cable access television.

Making it common knowledge that you adhere to a no excuse 24-hour rule when it comes to returning phone calls builds credibility quickly. Let your staff and community know that your rule is to return all phone calls within 24 hours after receiving them. In today's world of cell phones, it can be easier to follow this plan than it was just a few years ago. A very busy high school principal said, "My rule, when it comes to returning phone calls in a timely fashion, is that there are absolutely no excuses to fail to do so."

Since the challenges facing today's educational leaders can be quite similar, it is helpful to communicate with your colleagues, at least on a regional basis. It is also helpful to use e-mail, telephones, and meetings to communicate with those who are at a different level within the organization, as well as those who share the same job description and title. For example, an assistant principal could find it helpful to communicate with directors, principals, or other assistant principals.

Some leaders, in maintaining open lines of communication, keep a written journal of a running dialogue of events and how the events are perceived at different levels within and outside their organizations. Through reflection, this activity becomes developmental in nature, serving to enhance one's effectiveness in his or her current position, and is used to build on experiences in preparation for future assignments that will likely carry an increase in responsibility. "Journaling and reflection on my entries has become my primary staff development," was the feeling expressed by an elementary principal.

Communication is the most powerful leadership tool a superintendent can use in leading effectively. Having the ability to get others to understand you as completely as possible is an important aspect of your success. Having a strong network from which to receive and disseminate information is an excellent method for monitoring rumors and gossip. This network can and should also be used to receive early factual information.

Communicating with the board of education from the superintendent's office includes keeping board members informed, establishing and maintaining their trust, and appropriately including the board in decision-making. Involve the board and the staff in the development and understanding of district goals. Although for superintendents, in general, politics are always a challenge, board members are more likely to be receptive if the message from the superintendent is clear and consistent; if board members have been a part of the process, when appropriate; and if there are no surprises. One superintendent advises, "It's sometimes hard for me, but I try to place myself in the position of a board member. I don't always agree, but I am better able to understand where they are coming from."

Make certain that board members have ample opportunities to visit schools. If you are a superintendent visiting schools with the board, take time to interpret the mission and challenges. Communicate with media and politicians. Design a system that will guarantee that you receive important telephone calls rather than having them rerouted. Utilize parent surveys to help foster positive relationships between the district and parents. A seasoned superintendent captured his experiences when he said, "I will go to any extreme to make certain that I am getting factual and unfiltered information. I tell my staff to make certain that I hear the things they don't want me to hear."

NOTES:

_____

_____

Corollary 2
In times of uncertainty, a successful educational leader relies heavily on an informal network for understanding his/her organization and its environment. He/she maintains a network from the custodial staff to the business community elite.

The informal network is essential because people need a way to send and receive information that is too tenuous, complex, or political to be "on the record." Use the network as a broad forum for informally delivering early news about changes in policies or procedures and to get informal responses and feedback for developing ideas. Rely on informal conversations for much of the data about the "world" within which you act.

Every culture has "priests and priestesses" who "bless what goes on" and who "take confessions" regardless of what the leaders say is important. Use the informal network to identify the priests and priestesses in your school or district. You can shop potential ideas, seek help with special projects, or get reactions to potential personnel assignments. Leaders report that they often get some of their most useful information from chatting with custodial, transportation, and cafeteria staff members. Of course, there are limits to this approach. One district-level leader said, "I've learned over the years that it can be extremely beneficial to pay attention to the grapevine. Sometimes there's more to hang your hat on there than through the formal communication channels."

People want to help you do your job. Use the informal network to provide structure for managing special interest groups. Attack the "sacred cows" of your school or district by using outside groups. One superintendent used an outside consulting group to conduct a curriculum audit. The results of the audit showed that there were so many high school course offerings that it would take a high school student over 30 years to take everything offered. There were also five curriculum tracks. The point is that things had gotten out of hand; and, if the superintendent had attempted to dismantle some of the sacred cows without outside help, his tenure would have been short lived.

NOTES:

_____

_____

_____

_____

Corollary 3
The successful educational leader "lays bread crumb trails." He/she communicates the needs and concerns of the organization through concentration on a small number of issues and through the use of "controlled leaks" and repetition.

The idea of laying bread crumb trails has to do with floating information to identify initial reactions, both positive and negative. By actually controlling what is leaked, the educational leader can follow-up by seeking specific responses from those individuals who will hear about the issue. Through the process of squirting or leaking information, it is possible to get needed reactions from such groups as the board, media, local governing officials, the business community, teacher leaders, and other special interest groups. This feedback can be helpful as the educational leader moves toward a decision, especially a major decision.

When leaders lay a trail of information for those less intimately involved with an issue, they can help these stakeholders better understand the ramifications of the issue as the stakeholders assimilate their own patterns of understanding. As these patterns of understanding are created, even under significant time pressures, the stakeholders begin to feel a sense of ownership. Strategies used by leaders include the use of a master storyteller in the district who can pass on positive information about the culture of schools. Other leaders spend time educating the public on new state requirements and how they affect their schools or systems. This helps alleviate fear of the unknown. One practitioner said, "It seems that we can never get away from how we started in this profession; we're always teaching."

Although effective educational leaders prefer open communication, many find that leaking some information can be helpful to school principals when exploring changes in their schools. One principal was considering restructuring the school schedule and his first step was to share the possibility with his leadership team and then to take the team to visit two different schools. The teacher leaders had informal conversations with those in the schools being visited about team formation and teaching preferences. They began thinking about change and about how to solicit input from their colleagues.

Some district-level leaders send out feelers concerning major decisions that are pending, including major decisions about administrative appointments. This approach yields valuable information from parents, teachers, and the community. The key appears to be knowing how to do this in an effective manner and using this as just one of many communication strategies. When it comes to sending out feelers, one superintendent said, "I try to be as honest and forthright as I can without singling out personalities."

NOTES:

Corollary 4
Effective communicators understand that it is the quality rather than the quantity of information that creates the desired impact.

In constructing memos to your staff that contain general information, general instructions, policies, and procedures, it is best to be brief and concise. Our leaders believe that there is little more discouraging to very busy readers than pages of typed material. Sending precisely written communications to teachers and parents, including information about student discipline and how to help the students, can be positively received. The wholesale distribution of newsletters and other memoranda can fail to produce the results the leader intends.

Leaders find that key issues that are a part of the school or district culture; changes in guidelines; and issues around end-of-course testing, end-of-grade testing, and accountability standards are all topics of interest. However, when the guidelines around accountability standards change, it creates an appearance of inconsistency or constantly changing messages. It makes leaders uncomfortable when they have to communicate these on-going changes.

Many school principals see the need to share all the information they have available on a particular topic with their assistant principals. The principals cite that, when this is the case, often the assistant principals become a major support system for the principal. Other leaders see many special interest groups outside the system as wanting to help them do their jobs. One strategy for managing these groups includes sharing district goals and concerns with these special interest groups. In doing so, a deeper understanding of the bigger picture is created.

Leaders note that technology is a great tool for them. However, they caution to not "over communicate," especially with e-mail. They believe that, with the ease and speed of dissemination and with the communication advancements available, America overuses e-mail. Many leaders say they that they receive so many e-mail messages that they don't have time to read them, much less respond. One leader suggests that we adopt the definition of e-mail as emergencies only.

In general, leaders believe that, when others understand, they are more effective members of the organization. They not only better understand the goals and expectations of the leader; but, due to enhanced clarity, are able to more easily construct creative solutions to help achieve the goals. One superintendent with over a decade of experience said, "If you want others to be with you when the going gets tough, you better be an effective communicator; and you had better have been communicating effectively all along."

NOTES:

Corollary 5
The successful leader realizes that non-verbal communication is often more effective in sending a message than the spoken or written word.

The way you sit, stand, or walk sends a loud message — even more of a message sometimes than a wagging tongue. For example, a kind word uttered with a scornful face delivers a mixed message. If leaders are not good at using and interpreting non-verbal communication, training in this area should be a priority. One of our leaders suggested that if we want to determine how effective non-verbal communication can be, "Just take an opportunity to see a silent movie made back in the 1920's."

NOTES:

_____

_____

_____

_____

Corollary 6
Senior-level leaders and the leaders he/she leads need to conduct an honest evaluation of the effectiveness of meetings in carrying out school business.

The typical educator spends an inordinate amount of time attending scheduled or called meetings. The question to be asked is, "Is this time well spent?" Irrelevant topics and "bull sessions" should never appear on the agenda of a professional meeting. To the extent possible, meetings should be scheduled during normal working hours. When teachers are scheduled to attend meetings, always take into account the importance of minimizing interferences with teaching and learning. Make it a point to allow teachers to have some time in their classrooms even on professional development days, which are typically used for staff development activities. A young and inexperienced principal was quick to point out, "It didn't take long for me to find out that time in the classroom on teacher work days is something that is sacred."

Effective leaders avoid filling up the meeting agenda with items that can easily be handled with short memos and announcements. Discourage those in attendance at your meetings from bringing up personal issues that do not concern a large number of staff. Finally, cancel scheduled meetings when there are no important issues or topics to be presented or discussed. One leader indicated, "The best meeting I had was the one I cancelled."

NOTES:

_____

_____

_____

_____

**ASSESSMENT INSTRUMENT TO DETERMINE THE EXTENT
THAT YOU CURRENTLY EMPLOY OR HAVE IMPROVED IN THE USE OF
EFFECTIVE COMMUNICATION SKILLS AND PRACTICES**

Instructions: This instrument is designed to help you determine your current status and change in status relative to improvement in the use of effective communication skills and practices. Before reacting to the scale, decide whether you wish to appraise your current practices or the changes you have made in these practices over a particular period of time by circling either:

Current Status	*Rating*	*Change In Status*
Used to <u>very great</u> extent	5	Made <u>significant</u> positive change
Used to <u>great</u> extent	4	Made <u>some</u> positive change
Used to <u>moderate</u> extent	3	Made <u>little or no</u> change
Used to <u>a little</u> extent	2	Made <u>some</u> negative change
Used to <u>no</u> extent	1	Made <u>significant</u> negative change

Indicators of Effective Communications	**Rating**				
1. Strives to understand and use effective communication principles.	5	4	3	2	1
2. Keeps key stakeholders informed of current major problems and events – both good and bad – within the school.	5	4	3	2	1
3. Continues to communicate the mission and goals of the school.	5	4	3	2	1
4. Makes a major effort to inform the public of the importance of education in a democratic society.	5	4	3	2	1
5. Uses available network to communicate to the staff and general public.	5	4	3	2	1
6. Attempts to discourage rumors and gossip.	5	4	3	2	1
7. Keeps an open door to encourage legitimate dialogue.	5	4	3	2	1
8. Uses non-verbal methods of communicating effectively.	5	4	3	2	1
9. Conducts effective staff meetings.	5	4	3	2	1
10. Communicates through the use of brief and concise memos and directives.	5	4	3	2	1
11. Listens attentively to others who speak.	5	4	3	2	1
12. Provides training in effective communication skills.	5	4	3	2	1

ON THE JOB DEVELOPMENT PLANS AND ACTIVITIES
(COMMUNICATION)

Instructions: The purpose of this chart is to provide you with a simple way for you to list your strengths and developmental needs, prioritize your improvement objectives, and list strategies that you might use to reach your goals. Reflect on past experiences and review all personal assessment data, including the previous page, to complete this task.

Strengths	Developmental Needs

Improvement Objectives	Possible Strategies

"BACK HOME" APPLICATIONS
(Communication)

Instructions: Based on your understanding of the lesson and the corollaries, pick one or two of the skills and consider your previous experiences and possible future applications "back home" in your leadership role.

SKILL	PREVIOUS EXPERIENCE	FUTURE APPLICATIONS
Communicating Effectively, **Informal Networking,** **Creating/Leaking Trails of Information, and** **Effectiveness of Meetings**		

Lesson 5

ACCEPT THE FACT THAT YOU WILL ALWAYS HAVE TO CONTEND WITH OPPONENTS OF PUBLIC EDUCATION

- Decide to what extent you can change your detractors; and, if you can, develop viable strategies and use them. If not, don't waste any more of your time thinking about them.

- Work with your supporters (who are many) to promote education.

- By recognizing people who oppose education or oppose you philosophically, you will be able to put your energies where you can do the most good. When you develop a good staff and a good network of listeners, you will be effective and get the most accomplished. Be prepared to recognize goals met and share this recognition so that your "people" will redouble their efforts to help you succeed.

UNDERSTANDING THE LESSON

Many years ago I heard a speaker suggest that leaders should separate constituents into one of three categories: the "for's," the "agin's," and the "persuadables." The idea is that people are either supportive of what you are trying to accomplish; they are against your leadership agenda; or they have not yet made up their minds. If constituents are for your leadership agenda, then keep them informed through "executive" summaries. If they have not yet made up their minds, spend most of your time with them, trying to convince them to join your base of support. If someone is truly against you, don't waste time and energy trying to convince them to change their position and get behind your efforts.

Leaders say that they have learned that there are those who are contrarians just for the sake of being so. In situations such as this, make a strong effort early on to work with them, especially when your agenda includes promoting best practices. Taking on the responsibility for formally leading staff development activities, provides a setting for doing this. However, if you cannot get them to join in the direction, move on and surround yourself with people who are positive contributors to the goals that the school and district are trying to accomplish. A successful principal said, "I have only so much time and so much energy; I have to decide how I am going to spend it."

When staff members who are negative begin to "infect" other staff, leaders should employ whatever option is available to them under board policies and school laws. Staff members are sometimes encouraged to transfer out; they are forced out; or sometimes they maintain a physical presence, but are not expected to participate as a team member. In one situation, a negative teacher refused to participate as a member of a middle school grade-level team. She couldn't be fired and she wouldn't quit, so the rest of the team basically ignored her and moved ahead. This certainly was not ideal, but at least the entire team was not pulled down.

NOTES:

_____

_____

_____

_____

_____

_____

_____

_____

_____

_____

UNDERSTANDING THE COROLLARIES

Corollary 1
The successful educational leader strives to "see the same individuals in multiple contexts" to enhance decision-making and appropriate action. Ongoing contact with key influentials is one way that the leader can market his/her vision and program.

Leaders, especially superintendents, whose tenure exceeds the national average of time in a position, try to make decisions that, over time, make sense to a large and varied group of people. By having repeated contact with those individuals impacted by the decision, educational leaders are able to present a larger set of cues which helps reduce confusion, build trust, and prevent misunderstanding. Examples of opportunities for repeated contact include membership on civic club boards, working with the YMCA or YWCA, and participating in community leadership programs. One suburban superintendent said, "A large part of my job is to represent the district externally to the greater community. I grow weary of so many meetings; but, when it is crunch time, I can usually make a phone call to someone outside the system who is willing to help."

When leaders initially failed to learn the importance of this lesson, they later, through reflection, felt less prepared for their next position. They came to see that, if they can increase their involvement with key influentials and other individuals and community groups, they can expand their base of support for accomplishing much more for their organization. They also saw the added advantage of using these settings to address areas of concern.

At the district-level, it is important to associate with colleagues outside the central office setting. Leaders talk of the importance of being consistent in developing relationships throughout their organization and of finding multiple settings to work with people. Associating with colleagues in graduate school, associating with teachers at off-campus celebrations, and having lunch away from campus are ways of networking that also provide an arena for leaders to articulate their vision. Identifying key business partners and making contact with them frequently helps effect success in "marketing" one's vision and program. A district-level leader said, "It has become imperative to be willing and able to conduct business in more non-traditional settings. I've drunk a lot of coffee in the last three years."

Those who have an axe to grind will attempt to demand much of your attention, but this does not mean than they necessarily fall into the category of being your enemy. Leaders can make the distinction between the axe grinders and their true enemies and find it most important to know their enemies well. Leaders recognize that their friends and supporters and even those who may have an axe to grind will not attempt to invoke personal damage. This is not the case with true enemies. To be effective, leaders must keep their friends close, but they must keep their enemies closer.

In general, effective leaders attempt to "stay ahead" of issues and have plans in place to handle multiple situations. They work with their staffs on how and what types of decisions should be made and by whom. Leaders understand the importance of being viewed as consistent leaders in many contexts, and they send consistent messages throughout the organization over time. Be consistent in what you represent and how you present yourself before your many constituents. Always be aware of the particular audience with whom you are working, their interests, and their specific agenda. Then carefully promote your agenda, but in a genuine and sincere fashion. An effective leader said, "I respect each person's right to have an opinion, but I tell my story as well."

NOTES:

_____

_____

_____

_____

Corollary 2
A successful educational leader "manages premises rather than outcomes." Effective decision-makers make the fewest decisions, but they know which ones to make. Rather than making "all" the decisions, the leader provides guidance and often tries to shape the general direction of the decision.

In educational decision making, effective leaders act in more general terms. They exert their leadership by giving careful attention to committee membership, the timing of meetings, the content of agendas, and other devices that might shape the general nature of a decision. High leverage activities used by leaders include stressing the importance of such issues as strategic planning, advancing programs for at-risk populations, overall accountability, and recruitment of minority personnel. Leaders strive to employ competent people, paint them the broad important picture, and then empower them to "connect the dots." One building-level leader said, "The best boss I ever had never told me how to do a job, but shaped the general direction and spoke of the importance of outcomes."

District-level leaders see the importance of framing contexts and problems that allow space for others to be creative in seeking solutions. They recognize that it is not important for them as the formal leaders to have all the answers. However, they believe that posing the correct questions is an essential part of framing the context. Once the committee is selected, setting up a timetable can also become a strategy for shaping direction. An assistant superintendent said, "Remember, the outcomes don't have to be exactly what you would do; they can be similar and still work."

NOTES:

_____

_____

_____

_____

Corollary 3
Never put yourself into a position where you outwardly oppose the efforts of groups with vested interests as long as the groups' motives are to help even a small segment of the student population.

There are stakeholders who will devote an inordinate amount of time and energy on behalf of a few students. One example would be those supporters of programs for academically gifted students. The leader's job is to encourage this interest; but, at the same time, to persuade these people to look at the bigger picture. A possible strategy is to identify all the major special interest groups in your school or district and briefly define their "demands." As these various groups exert pressure, provide them a brief handout listing the concerns of all the special interest groups.

School superintendents spend considerable time with special interest groups. One superintendent stated that, when he is in a meeting with a special interest group, he becomes the "best listener the world has ever seen." He uses the same response over and over, "I commend you for your interest and assure you that I will weigh your concerns and needs along with the concerns and needs of other groups." This approach tends to work well most of the time. Identifying, recruiting, and employing staff members who have expertise that allows them to better understand and communicate with special interest groups is another strategy used by some superintendents.

Finally, our leaders note that they will not stay leaders for very long if they try to please everyone. They make decisions that tend to benefit the majority while attempting to maintain trust through being honest and preventing misunderstandings as much as possible.

NOTES:

_____

_____

_____

_____

Corollary 4
To no one's surprise, those in society who have the greatest needs are those who have the least power and influence. In a democracy, a good leader becomes the advocate for the needy, who have no clout.

The lowest achieving students in schools generally come from disadvantaged, low-income families who are virtually powerless in influencing policy and financial appropriations. Leaders at all levels need to assure that these individuals get their "slice of the pie." Also, most of the recent state and federal accountability legislation is designed to assure that students attain established minimum standards. A large proportion of the students who do not meet these standards come from low-income families. An appropriate reaction to this situation by school leaders is, "We endorse the establishment of standards and stand ready to be accountable, but we must have the resources to carry out this mandate."

It is often difficult for leaders to balance the needs of the neediest with the interests of the less needy. One leader said, "If I could spend half the time that I devote listening to the concerns of soccer moms with improving student performance for poor kids, I'd get an award." Another described an encounter with a parent that was highly volatile. She stood her ground on a discipline decision and the meeting turned "ugly." However, following the meeting, the students involved behaved well at school and on the bus. The parent became more involved with the school; and, through interaction with the principal, gained respect and understanding. The principal concludes that, because she did not waiver on the discipline decision, the parent gained respect for all she does for all children. These multiple and varied interactions with the parent allowed for better rapport.

NOTES:

_____

_____

_____

_____

ASSESSMENT INSTRUMENT TO DETERMINE THE EXTENT YOU CURRENTLY EMPLOY OR HAVE IMPROVED IN YOUR ABILITY TO USE STRATEGIES TO WORK WITH OPPONENTS OF PUBLIC EDUCATION

Instructions: This instrument is designed to help you determine your current status and change in status relative to working with those who oppose or do not care about education or special interest groups. Before reacting to the scale, decide whether you wish to appraise your current practices or the changes you have made in these practices over a particular period of time.

Current Status	*Rating*	*Change In Status*
Uses to <u>very great</u> extent	5	Made <u>significant</u> positive change
Uses to <u>great</u> extent	4	Made <u>some</u> positive change
Uses to <u>moderate</u> extent	3	Made <u>little or no</u> change
Uses to <u>a little</u> extent	2	Made <u>some</u> negative change
Uses to <u>no</u> extent	1	Made <u>significant</u> negative change

Indicators of Effectiveness in Working with Detractors and Special Interest Groups	**Rating**				
1. Is aware of detractors and their motives/agendas.	5	4	3	2	1
2. Ignores groups that refuse to debate or negotiate.	5	4	3	2	1
3. Embraces and works with supporters of education.	5	4	3	2	1
4. Develops strategies for getting groups with vested interests to see the "big picture."	5	4	3	2	1
5. Makes decisions and takes action in the best interests of the most students.	5	4	3	2	1
6. Is tactful and understanding in conferring with individuals who do not support the school's mission.	5	4	3	2	1
7. Defines tasks and jobs in general terms while delegating the responsibility for details to subordinates.	5	4	3	2	1
8. Devotes time to making major decisions; does not "major in minors."	5	4	3	2	1
9. Has a clear picture of the objectives of legitimate pressure groups and uses this information to advocate balanced programs.	5	4	3	2	1
10. Serves as an advocate for powerless groups.	5	4	3	2	1
11. Recommends school board policies that assist in working with distracters.	5	4	3	2	1
12. Uses key staff members, who have entrée with special groups, to influence and negotiate.	5	4	3	2	1

ON THE JOB DEVELOPMENT PLANS AND ACTIVITIES
(OPPONENTS OF PUBLIC EDUCATION)

Instructions: The purpose of this chart is to provide you with a simple way for you to list your strengths and developmental needs, prioritize your improvement objectives, and list strategies that you might use to reach your goals. Reflect on past experiences and review all personal assessment data, including the previous page, to complete this task.

Strengths	Developmental Needs

Improvement Objectives	Possible Strategies

"BACK HOME" APPLICATIONS
(Opponents of Public Education)

Instructions: Based on your understanding of the lesson and the corollaries, pick one or two of the skills and consider your previous experiences and possible future applications "back home" in your leadership role.

SKILL	PREVIOUS EXPERIENCE	FUTURE APPLICATIONS
Contending with Those Who Oppose Public Education,		
Repeated Contact in Multiple Settings,		
Shaping Decision, and		
Advocating for the Most Needy		

Lesson 6

ALTHOUGH A NUMBER OF SCHOOL LEADERS (PRIMARILY SUPERINTENDENTS) HAVE PROBLEMS IN WORKING WITH THEIR BOARDS OF EDUCATION, SCHOOL BOARDS ARE ONE OF THE BEST EXAMPLES OF DEMOCRACY IN ACTION AND CAN BE A STRONG ASSET IN OPERATING THE SCHOOLS.

- Strive to get your board members to understand their roles as policy makers and not administrators. Use outside consultants, if necessary, to make this point.

- Alert school board members of major potential problems and issues as soon as they are identified. No surprises!

- Never take sides when there is a split in the board due to personality differences. When called upon to make recommendations, make them strictly on the merits of the situation.

UNDERSTANDING THE LESSON

Working with school boards in a productive manner is extremely challenging and requires that leaders take a team approach if they are going to be effective. It is critical that accurate information consistently flows to the board and that central office staff and principals serve as valuable resource people in assisting the superintendent in working with the board. Typically, superintendents use school board updates to communicate with their boards on such issues as personnel matters, financial matters, and legislative interpretations. School superintendents seem to adopt the philosophy expressed by the superintendent who said, "It has been my experience that it pays to give the board as much information as they can possibly deal with."

When board membership changes, it is always a good idea to conduct formal orientation sessions for the new board members. Although many states offer orientations for new board members through their state associations, the sessions are typically more generic and do not focus directly on specific local issues that may be of interest to your board. The state association sessions can certainly prove helpful; but, when you can conduct a local orientation, it helps educate the new members about their roles, provides an arena for advancing the major themes of the school district, and allows the superintendent to share his/her vision for the district. Many superintendents use their multiple contacts with their boards to repeat themes that they feel are important and are a part of their plan for the district. Some common themes include increasing student achievement, decreasing dropouts, and closing the achievement gap.

Although there are circumstances that are sometimes out of the control of superintendents and other educational leaders, the price for galvanizing and alienating board members may be a contract buy out. School principals who have learned lessons from observing their superintendents work with boards find that, when this relationship is less than positive, often the board will attempt to micromanage the school system. The principal of a large elementary school in an affluent community said, "My superintendent earns his salary if he doesn't do anything but manage the board."

NOTES:

_____

_____

_____

_____

_____

_____

_____

_____

_____

UNDERSTANDING THE COROLLARIES

Corollary 1
Effective leadership requires creating connections. Effective leaders involve people in solving common problems.

Involving people and networking are obviously vital leadership tools. Getting citizens in the community involved in educational affairs; mingling with staff, especially teachers; getting to know and work with stakeholders; soliciting the aid of politicians and other decision-makers; working with adversaries; and attending local, state, and national conferences moves the informal network to the next level, the level of connections.

Practitioners use many strategies for building connections. Encouraging school boards to hold public meetings to obtain input on the creation of the budget, discussing major education issues, involving low-income parents in the academic affairs of their students, creating a cross section of parents to serve on a parent advisory council to advise principals on important issues, and involving critics, as well as supporters as a part of the team are examples of strategies that work. Embedded in each of these strategies is the leader's desire to understand what drives the different groups of stakeholders. Leaders at the building level express the feelings of the principal who said, "We must explain the reasons behind our actions and involve those directly affected by the outcomes."

Teacher empowerment has been among the approaches used by educational leaders for many years. Leaders report that teacher empowerment has an important place in today's educational world. Teachers help prepare budgets; they construct supply orders and receive exactly what they order as long as the money lasts. Teachers assume the responsibility, through social and other committees, for keeping staff members informed of illnesses, births, and deaths of relatives of faculty and staff.

In order that a structure might be created for expressing teacher concerns, teacher committees are formed to meet regularly with principals and district-level leaders. Although this structure is generally effective, our leaders report that it requires skill to keep this from becoming nothing more than a complaint group. A building-level leader said, "In our school, we must provide leadership and team training if we want our teachers to become all that they can become."

Again, at the building level, school-centered decision making creates the dynamics that lead to team building and an enhanced climate that supports building connections. Leaders view this approach to be healthy in that it shares some of the politics involved in running a school by providing a mechanism for influencing program decisions. School principals build upon this approach as a forum for articulating and establishing a clear understanding of their visions and goals for their schools. Other examples of building connections through an informal network include community contacts made through involvement with local athletic programs. This may result in financial contributions that can assist with facilities construction and the purchase of equipment.

NOTES:

_____

_____

_____

_____

Corollary 2
The successful educational leader "rehearses and repeats explanations" so that he/she can work out the details of his/her "message" and then communicate the message in a way that it becomes familiar to all stakeholders. He/she recognizes that less is really more.

Rehearsals help bring order and enhance the possibility of creating a better understanding of complex issues. Rehearsals involve playing out an issue in one's mind and practicing explaining the issue in ways that allow for deeper exploration. The process of rehearsal with your staff requires that mechanisms be established that allow for explanations and the expression of ideas in a free-flowing and non-threatening or "off the record" environment. "It is during these rehearsals that I insist on honest, open, and direct feedback - no apple polishing allowed," said one superintendent.

Rehearsing and repeating explanations is akin to playing "what if" and is frequently used by leaders and their staffs in preparation for all kinds of public presentations, especially board meetings. Other rehearsals include preparing for a student function such as National Honor Society induction ceremonies, school showcasing, and meeting with parents to discuss difficult situations involving their children.

Many leaders indicate that it has been their standard practice to rehearse in preparation for speeches and for conducting workshops. Rehearsals enhance their ability for quick thinking and enable them to gain confidence in dealing with their constituents. By rehearsing in front of a mirror, leaders are able to watch their general body language, including hand gestures, facial expressions, and the amount of head and eye movement. In rehearsing, leaders get better at anticipating questions that might be raised by their audience and are then able to preplan hypothetical responses.

Leaders tend to utilize themes that drive their reasoning and action. A repetition of the leader's themes and explanations helps constituents have a better understanding of issues. The more complex the issue, the more "lead time" you need in working with your constituents. This builds a team approach to problem solving and creates a shared responsibility for outcomes by bringing multiple people on board who begin to feel ownership.

NOTES:

Corollary 3
The successful educational leader is politically astute. He/she understands that the successful use of political skills is absolutely necessary to build and maintain a power base of allies who will support his/her initiatives to advance the interests of the school system.

Bureaucracies exist to satisfy some of the needs of the leading social strata. There are significant political implications about this phenomenon. School systems, as public bureaucracies, cannot escape the scrutiny of all those who have a vested interest. When it comes to political skills, a long-time district-level leader said, "If you're not comfortable with politics or if you can't get comfortable in a hurry, your tenure in educational leadership will be short."

These interested parties not only attempt to influence, but frequently do, in fact, influence the direction of the system, even if leaders at all levels might prefer otherwise. In this context, leaders use political strategies to advance the idea of a shared responsibility and a shared accountability for the outcomes produced by their schools and districts. Special interest groups whose views differ from those of the leaders often cause a re-examination of perspectives. This re-examination can result in a new direction that is more in keeping with the interests of stakeholder groups and, in turn, can create support and ownership for the initiative. This successful involvement of stakeholders will be enhanced if the leaders are committed to a "larger agenda."

Politically astute leaders work on a problem rather than actually solving the problem. Working on the problem often means leaving details open, as political realities tend to shape the decisions to be made. One leader stated, "I'm not a political animal, but I realize that, if I am going to survive in the blackboard jungle, I have to wrestle with alligators." Another leader recommends that you accept the fact that your distracters are not your enemies and that you strive to make them your negotiating partners. Frequently, leaders are able to reach beyond their original expectations because of additional insights that are gained from working on the problem.

Superintendents are advised to help board members understand their roles as policy makers and to keep board members informed, always avoiding surprises. Never take sides with one board member over another; educate the board on important issues; and keep accurate information flowing with regularity. Each premise helps ensure success through maintaining positive board relations. Superintendents can create buy-in through both formal and informal contacts and maintaining ethical practices at all times.

Superintendents should not "get caught in the middle" between board members and should also recognize that the power of the board is with the board as an entity, not with individual members.

Leadership occurs when leaders develop a sense of knowing when to hold on to their recommendation and when to let go. This becomes clearer when leaders work to empower others. The act of empowerment causes all parties to feel valued and results in better working relationships that lead to better solutions. One leader said, "Give power away." Giving power away causes leaders to become more effective when they realize that not everything has to be done by the leader himself or herself.

NOTES:

_____

_____

_____

_____

Corollary 4
The wise educational leader uses school board policies as a doctor would use preventive medicine. The superintendent anticipates future problems and urges the board to adopt policies that will block them – or if they do occur, deflate them.

A common problem associated with school board policy is that many districts have too many policies. The elimination of outdated and irrelevant policies will do much to enhance the administration of schools. One school superintendent, who inherited a full-time staff attorney said, "I offered to pay the board attorney not to write so many policies."

Periodic needs assessments should be conducted to identify future potential problems and the desirability of creating "preventive" policies. In an effort to block a national soft drink company from placing soft drink machines in school cafeterias, one superintendent got his board to pass a policy requiring the local health department "to establish criteria for approving the food and drink served in the lunchrooms." However, the development of policy for blocking legitimate debate and the exercise of constitutional rights should not be tolerated.

NOTES:

_____

_____

_____

_____

ASSESSMENT INSTRUMENT TO DETERMINE THE EXTENT YOU ARE OR HAVE IMPROVED IN WORKING EFFECTIVELY WITH YOUR SCHOOL BOARD

Instructions: This instrument is designed to help you determine your current status and change in status relative to working effectively with your board. Before reacting to the scale, decide whether you wish to appraise your current practices or the changes you have made in these practices over a particular period of time.

Current Status	*Rating*	*Change In Status*
Uses to <u>very great</u> extent	5	Made <u>significant</u> positive change
Uses to <u>great</u> extent	4	Made <u>some</u> positive change
Uses to <u>moderate</u> extent	3	Made <u>little or no</u> change
Uses to <u>a little</u> extent	2	Made <u>some</u> negative change
Uses to <u>no</u> extent	1	Made <u>significant</u> negative change

Indicators of Working Effectively With Your Board of Education	Rating
1. Strives to get board members to understand role as policymakers.	5 4 3 2 1
2. Alerts board of major potential problems as soon as they occur.	5 4 3 2 1
3. Makes recommendations based on the merit of the situation or the best interest of students.	5 4 3 2 1
4. Remains neutral when there is a split in the board due to personality differences.	5 4 3 2 1
5. Works with and through the board of education to make community connections in solving problems.	5 4 3 2 1
6. Rehearses critical presentations to board and public to assure understanding and positive reaction.	5 4 3 2 1
7. Repeats (hammers home) critical assets, needs, and problems that must to be communicated.	5 4 3 2 1
8. Exhibits political savvy with the board and community.	5 4 3 2 1
9. Uses the board to assist in identifying the needs and concerns of various stakeholders.	5 4 3 2 1
10. Encourages the school board to adopt policy that will block and/or cushion potential problems.	5 4 3 2 1
11. Conducts periodic reviews of policy to identify gaps and weed out outdated or irrelevant items.	5 4 3 2 1
12. Assures that school board policies are adopted which are consistent with the best interests of students.	5 4 3 2 1

ON THE JOB DEVELOPMENT PLANS AND ACTIVITIES
(WORKING EFFECTIVELY WITH YOUR SCHOOL BOARD)

Instructions: The purpose of this chart is to provide you with a simple way for you to list your strengths and developmental needs, prioritize your improvement objectives, and list strategies that you might use to reach your goals. Reflect on past experiences and review all personal assessment data, including the previous page, to complete this task.

Strengths	Developmental Needs

Improvement Objectives	Possible Strategies

"BACK HOME" APPLICATIONS
(Working Effectively with Your School Board)

Instructions: Based on your understanding of the lesson and the corollaries, pick one or two of the skills and consider your previous experiences and possible future applications "back home" in your leadership role.

SKILL	*PREVIOUS EXPERIENCE*	*FUTURE APPLICATIONS*
Board of Education as an Asset,		
Creating Connections,		
Rehearsing Explanations,		
Political Astuteness, and		
Board Policy		

Lesson 7

YOUR JOB AS A SCHOOL LEADER IS IMPORTANT, BUT KEEP ITS IMPORTANCE IN PERSPECTIVE – YOUR LIFE IS, TOO!

- Take time to be with your family, become involved in regular exercise and recreational activities, and take time to look at and "smell the roses." And, by all means, develop a sense of humor.

UNDERSTANDING THE LESSON

A large number of our leaders indicate that the hardest thing for them to do is to find reasonable life balance. Leaders, in general, tend to be driven to achievement. Many are just not driven; they are seeking perfection. In so doing, they often sacrifice time with their families and ignore those behaviors that can lead to healthful living. High achieving leaders tend to be workaholics. Although they have been shaped in ways that contribute to their behavior both at work and at home, factors, such as too few professional support staff, lack of clerical support, and having to work with inexperienced assistants, inhibits life balance.

School superintendents who tend to be less out of balance have mastered perspective on their role and have learned to delegate accordingly. While they find the job extremely consuming, they have found renewal experiences outside of work that contribute to their relaxation, happiness, and which help them maintain their overall stamina. Some readers may find it somewhat surprising, but frequently leaders found that pursuing advanced degrees to be a professionally renewing experience. Other leaders found that spending time with their families could be extremely rejuvenating. Some leaders choose quietness for solitude, some choose to read a good book, others enjoy a ballgame, and some find it renewing to spend time with a special pet. Leaders are encouraged to remember the maxim, "I gave at the office," and find whatever activity it takes for personal renewal.

One leader stated:

> I have learned that work is work. I should enjoy it, but it's not my life. It's where I go to make money and, hopefully, make someone's life a little easier. My self-worth should not be tied in to how good or how bad a job I do, but it should be based on the factors that make me a person—how I treat others, how I interact with my family, my spiritual life, and who I am when the lights go down and I'm by myself.

A district-level leader said, "It's just a job; it's not my life." Another said, "If you enjoy what you're doing, you'll never work another day in your life."

NOTES:

_____

_____

_____

_____

_____

_____

_____

_____

_____

_____

UNDERSTANDING THE COROLLARIES

Corollary 1
Renewal means taking charge of your own development. Self-understanding is the key.

It has been my experience that the higher you move in the organization, the more difficult it becomes to access the kind of professional development activities that can directly impact on your growth as a leader. This means that leaders must ultimately take charge of their own development. To take charge means, that, fundamentally, leaders acquire an in-depth understanding of themselves. With self-understanding as the cornerstone for taking charge of one's development, leaders identified a wide range of activities and personal characteristics that help them with their ongoing development. These activities and personal characteristics include prayer, having a good sense of humor, networking with other leaders, family time, taking advantage of training opportunities, listening and understanding the nature of criticism, working with mentors, serving as mentors, reading, and attending conferences.

Among those activities cited by leaders as being helpful in taking charge of one's own development, many were activities outside of work. The three R's of reading, recreation, and reflecting received high marks. Leaders talked of activities that tend to "cleanse and renew." Spending time with one's spouse or significant other, beginning a regular exercise routine, joining and becoming active in professional organizations, attending conferences, and blocking out time for recreational activities were helpful. Taking a walk and absorbing the beauty of one's surroundings, listening to the birds sing, composing poetry, and developing the ability to see the humor in events that would have once been overwhelming were take-charge activities that are conducive to growth and development.

Quotes from our leaders included such comments as: "I have found being alone is great therapy for me." "Bad things happen. Once I accepted this fact, I've begun to see humor in events that, in my early days, overwhelmed me. Now I almost welcome problems." "Faith carries me through."

NOTES:

_____

_____

_____

Corollary 2
Research has demonstrated that people who maintain a high level of physical fitness are more productive and happier on the job.

Physically-fit people are generally more mentally alert and have more endurance than their less fit counterparts. In the main, physically-fit individuals have better posture and make a better appearance than those who don't exercise. Maintaining appropriate levels of physical fitness has become a way of life for many educational leaders. Comments include, "I don't hesitate to take time off from the job to workout. I've made it a part of my job description." Another leader stated, "Hitting a golf ball is better than hitting a distracter and a golf ball never hits back." Leaders also see the importance of physical fitness for their administrative team. One leader said, "I encourage my administrative team to stay physically fit by telling them how important it is to our operation." Our leaders warn that, when we show signs of stress, others feed off of it; to avoid sickness and becoming ineffective as a leader, build in recreation time.

Choosing educational leadership as a profession has always carried with it a certain amount of stress. However, with the advent of increased accountability, more stress has become a part of the leader's job at all levels of the school organization. The presence of increased stress has caused leaders to neglect themselves, their health, and often their family members while trying to do the job. Leaders encourage a certain amount of "selfishness" in order to improve one's chances for being a more well-rounded and balanced person. This often means building a time into your schedule to work on physical fitness.

NOTES:

_____

_____

_____

_____

Corollary 3
Having a high energy level and the good health to implement it is critical to your success.

It seems that high energy and good health go hand in hand. The quality of a leader's work life is in no small part based on having plenty of energy and being in good health as one faces the leadership challenges in today's educational organizations. Having a high energy level seems to make people more successful and success seems to energize people. Leaders with high energy levels tend to be happier, smile more, and are more optimistic than those with less energy. When conducting interviews for job vacancies, leaders speak of the importance of being on the lookout for signals that will provide insight as to whether or not the prospective candidate is energetic and in good health. The human resources director of a medium-size school district said, "My team and I are always looking for tell-tale signs of the candidates' overall physical, mental, and emotional well-being. We ask direct questions about exercise, hobbies, and their life in general."

NOTES:

_____

_____

_____

_____

Corollary 4
Depend on inner strength and a "power" outside yourself to sustain you.

Faith and prayer have carried many embattled leaders through personal and job-related trials and tribulations. Belief in God or a supreme being serves as the guide to renewal in the lives of many leaders. Leaders who look for a power outside of themselves to sustain them are quick to share that they don't want to get so big that they, in a figurative sense, become bigger than God. They don't want to confuse who they are as human beings with what they do as formal leaders. For many, the church or synagogue of choice has become a safe haven from the troubled waters that battle even the strongest of leaders. Their respective places of worship provide an environment that helps leaders forget job-related problems and, in turn, receive hope and strength.

Relying on daily prayer helps leaders stay focused and causes them to look at others and the challenges they face in a different light. Through prayer, leaders are able to focus on their strengths, manage their weaknesses, and better utilize humor to take a negative situation and turn it into something positive. By depending on inner strength and a power outside themselves, leaders can take better care of themselves emotionally, physically, and spiritually.

NOTES:

_____

_____

_____

_____

ASSESSMENT INSTRUMENT TO DETERMINE THE EXTENT THAT YOU CURRENTLY OR HAVE IMPROVED IN MAINTAINING A BALANCED WORK AND PERSONAL LIFE

Instructions: This instrument is designed to help you determine your current status and change in status relative to maintaining a balanced work and personal life. Before reacting to the scale, decide whether you wish to appraise your current practices or the changes you have made in these practices over a particular period of time.

Current Status	*Rating*	*Change In Status*
Uses to <u>very great</u> extent	5	Made <u>significant</u> positive change
Uses to <u>great</u> extent	4	Made <u>some</u> positive change
Uses to <u>moderate</u> extent	3	Made <u>little or no</u> change
Uses to <u>a little</u> extent	2	Made <u>some</u> negative change
Uses to <u>no</u> extent	1	Made <u>significant</u> negative change

Indicators of Maintaining Balanced Work/Personal Life	**Rating**				
1. Recognizes own needs and sources of strength that can be found in various aspects of life	5	4	3	2	1
2. Maintains a balance between the work and off-the-job portions of life.	5	4	3	2	1
3. Sees humor in both desirable and undesirable aspects of life.	5	4	3	2	1
4. Becomes involved in activities that enhance physical fitness and vigor.	5	4	3	2	1
5. Encourages staff to exercise and become involved in recreational activities.	5	4	3	2	1
6. Schedules quality time to be with family.	5	4	3	2	1
7. Depends on outer sources, as well as inner sources for strength.	5	4	3	2	1
8. Becomes involved in social and enrichment activities in the community.	5	4	3	2	1
9. Provides staff development programs to promote the maintenance of a balanced work/personal life.	5	4	3	2	1
10. Sets good example for workaholics and overly conscientious workers.	5	4	3	2	1
11. Takes advantage of allotted vacation days.	5	4	3	2	1
12. Believes in the old saying "that all work and no play make a dull boy."	5	4	3	2	1

ON THE JOB DEVELOPMENT PLANS AND ACTIVITIES
(MAINTAINING A BALANCED WORK AND PERSONAL LIFE)

Instructions: The purpose of this chart is to provide you with a simple way for you to list your strengths and developmental needs, prioritize your improvement objectives, and list strategies that you might use to reach your goals. Reflect on past experiences and review all personal assessment data, including the previous page, to complete this task.

Strengths	Developmental Needs

Improvement Objectives	Possible Strategies

"BACK HOME" APPLICATIONS
(Maintaining a Balanced Work and Personal Life)

Instructions: Based on your understanding of the lesson and the corollaries, pick one or two of the skills and consider your previous experiences and possible future applications "back home" in your leadership role.

SKILL	*PREVIOUS EXPERIENCE*	*FUTURE APPLICATIONS*
Importance of Life Outside of Work, **Taking Charge of Your Own Development,** **Maintaining Physical Fitness,** **High Energy Level and Good Health, and** **Inner Strength and Power Outside Yourself**		

Lesson 8

AS A SCHOOL LEADER, YOU CANNOT BE ALL THINGS TO ALL PEOPLE, NOR CAN SCHOOLS SOLVE ALL OF SOCIETY'S PROBLEMS.

- Define the mission of public education and your role in accomplishing its purpose. Refuse to accept responsibilities that are incompatible with the mission. Set priorities relative to the most important tasks that will be undertaken by you and the schools.

Understanding the Lesson

To be successful, experience teaches us that leaders should focus on three to five key areas for leading improvement with no more than three goals under each key area. Less is more in regard to choosing what is truly important in creating and maintaining an efficient and effective school or school system. Leaders must have their "hands in a lot of pots," but then leave the cooking to others. Good leaders are consummate generalists who hire competent people and then delegate effectively. Pace yourself and don't make promises that can't be kept. Keep your personal involvement in direct decision-making to a minimum, and always keep in mind the driving forces behind your agenda. One leader with a national reputation in school leadership said, "If you try to be everything to everyone, you will never get anything of importance accomplished. Less is more."

NOTES:

_____

_____

_____

_____

UNDERSTANDING THE COROLLARIES

Corollary 1
The successful leader develops clear and consistent "themes and agendas" in responding to many different issues. These themes and agendas help the members of an organization better understand and adjust to the intended outcomes.

Keep what is most important to you, what you value, in front of your constituents as you respond to your many challenges. For example, one often cited theme was how important decisions will impact on the welfare of students. Since it is important that your staff be able to predict, in so far as possible, how you will behave in any given situation or with any particular set of circumstances, keep your agenda in front of them as much as possible. Repeating one's priorities over and over can help organizational members develop a deeper understanding of what you value. Leaders' priorities often include such concerns as the central office being more of a service organization, accountability, and addressing the needs of at-risk student population. A major challenge for leaders in this process is developing the ability to simplify issues. The better a leader understands the complexities of a particular challenge, the more difficult it becomes to simplify the challenge for all stakeholders.

One superintendent noted that a constant revisiting of important themes and agendas for the school district help to ingrain the key issues that are the focus for the district. As this superintendent adds additional leadership positions to his staff, he sees the importance of being able to articulate his key themes of narrowing the achievement gap, equity among schools, and not getting side tracked with conflicting issues and special interest groups. Another district-level leader points out that, in order for the school district to move forward, clear goals and expectations must be developed. Then, she suggests, "These expectations must be broken down into smaller segments. It is through this approach that school improvement plans can be systematically developed." An effort is made to coordinate themes so more goals can fit with a small number of themes.

Developing themes is necessary for implementing the vision of the leader. The theme approach allows for a systemic approach to leading change and, at the center, is the leader's set of core beliefs which are applied in all situations. A pattern for problem solving is established and leaders become content with partial solutions when they use repetition to communicate a common set of themes that are value driven. In other words, leaders have so many balls in the air, it is rare that they can take any single issue from the beginning of a recognition point to an absolute solution. They, then, must be content with achieving partial solutions to any challenge and turning it loose for a while, going on to the next challenge, and then coming back to their earlier challenge.

At the school level, principals often review the school's purpose at each faculty meeting. This is preceded by having established themes for the school at the beginning of the school year. The principals and faculties refer back to the original themes on a monthly basis to see if revisions should be made. Leaders feel that it is vital that all parties feel that they can influence the direction of the school.

Similar to this approach is the approach used by other building-level administrators which consists of developing a list of goals for the school year and then keeping those goals in front of the teachers and parents. These building-level leaders continue to remind staff and parents of the targets that everyone is aspiring to achieve and how all share in a joint responsibility to accomplish the goals. This enables all stakeholders to share in working on "parts" of problems.

NOTES:

_____

_____

_____

Corollary 2
The successful educational leader understands that getting to closure on an issue requires "processing" the issue and usually results in incomplete solutions. His/her perception of issues is almost always bigger than the ability to act on issues and, thus, he/she must often be content to work on a small part of the larger whole.

Individuals and sub-groups within schools and school systems have different "processing" needs when it comes to problem solving. These differences create timeline issues since some people are pushing for closure and others are not. It is important to remember that lack of closure is an issue for all leaders and that it is okay to have partial closure.

Effective school leaders remember that they "work on" and "within" systems, and it is not possible to "tinker" with one segment or subsystem without there being implications for all parts of the system. With this in mind, processing issues or maintaining some discontinuity and developing a tolerance for ambiguity can provide for increased understanding and new ideas. Leaders always reflect on the systematic implications of such approaches, however, and know when it is important to act decisively. Leaders cannot possibly satisfy everyone, so they must stay focused on their mission and vision and use it to filter their behaviors. Leaders recommend developing clear themes based on accurate information, remembering that schools cannot solve all of society's problems. The principal of a small primary school said, "Try to always make the welfare of the students paramount in decision making."

When it comes to initiating change, many leaders say that they initiate changes that they know they may not see come to fruition, prior to their possibly leaving their positions. However, they outline the purpose and mission of the school or district, use clear and consistent language, plan strategically, and work to solve pieces of problems while understanding that the whole problem solution takes much longer.

NOTES:

_____

_____

_____

Corollary 3
Educational leaders must assume proactive, as well as reactive roles in solving educational problems.

School superintendents and other school leaders have played a minor role in recent decisions to reform education. Politicians have assumed a major role. Leaders generally feel that educators have surrendered the concept of local control, site-based management, and grassroots decision-making to state and national politicians. One leader said, "As soon as I think I have a handle on the newest mandate from the state or national government, along comes some new legislation." Another stated, "I'm impressed with the power and influence that some of the state teacher unions are exerting. Although I'm opposed to educators becoming involved in unions, we could emulate some their methods."

School principals feel that there is a prevailing attitude that, as an educational leader, you are to act in everyone's specific interest to solve their particular problems. They believe that, in many ways, principals try to be all things to all people, though it is an impossible task. A strategy used by some is to redirect constituents to the grassroots of their problem and help them begin brainstorming solutions. Constituents get some of their needs met and also become more self-reliant. When the demands get too great, principals use the mission of the school to move back to a more level playing field. They pose questions around correlates of the mission, such as, "What is instructionally sound? Does what is being asked of them meet the needs of the students? Is it efficient? Is it fiscally sound?"

Sound advice for superintendents and other school leaders is to become assertive in defining the mission of the schools. Try to always emphasize that the total staff should be working to accomplish the same goals and that everyone is working to serve students in the best way possible.

NOTES:

_____

_____

_____

_____

Corollary 4
To a great extent, educational leaders can do a better job of using existing leadership and management tools to assure that education focuses on the proper mission of the schools.

School board policy, the involvement of stakeholders, and comprehensive school planning are all tools that can be used to enhance leadership and management. School board policy can serve as an excellent tool for keeping the school's programs and activities moving in the proper direction. The involvement of stakeholders in defining mission and goals, and limitations of the school can help education remain on target. Comprehensive school improvement planning provides educators with a tool to systematically define realistic goals and establish meaningful priorities. A district-level leader noted, "Setting reasonable and relevant goals and priorities has not only reduced my work load, it has made me more efficient."

Learning how to break large issues into smaller more manageable pieces will allow one to more easily see progress. This is not a substitute for systems leadership, but it does produce a viable option for incremental improvements. In using this approach, leaders delegate more, utilize others who are influential in the district or school, and keep lines of communication open. Leaders hire good people, give them basic guidelines, and allow them to complete the tasks with little or no direct supervision. This demonstrates trust in the abilities and talents of those under their supervision. When the tasks are completed, leaders give those who completed the tasks the credit.

At the building level, school principals take into account the school climate and how their perceptions about low morale can negatively impact on the performance of teachers and students. Principals create school spirit teams to focus on positive things that are happening, both professionally and personally, with the inhabitants of the school. The spirit teams also plan social functions. These cultural attributes tend to increase teacher morale and create a positive climate for learning.

Conversations that matter take place in well-led schools. These conversations may be about how one person's inappropriate actions affect everyone else and may result in the gaining of new knowledge from simply taking time to share personal concerns. Involvement seems to motivate performance to higher levels and is an uplifting experience. A central office leader said, "People are still interested in how much you care about them as human beings."

NOTES:

ASSESSMENT INSTRUMENT TO DETERMINE THE EXTENT THAT YOU CURRENTLY OR HAVE IMPROVED IN FOCUSING ON THE "TRUE" MISSION OF THE SCHOOL

Instructions: This instrument is designed to help you determine your current status and change in status relative to focusing on the "true" mission of the school. Before reacting to the scale, decide whether you wish to appraise your current practices or the changes you have made in these practices over a particular period of time.

Current Status	*Rating*	*Change In Status*
Uses to <u>very great</u> extent	5	Made <u>significant</u> positive change
Uses to <u>great</u> extent	4	Made <u>some</u> positive change
Uses to <u>moderate</u> extent	3	Made <u>little or no</u> change
Uses to <u>a little</u> extent	2	Made <u>some</u> negative change
Uses to <u>no</u> extent	1	Made <u>significant</u> negative change

Indicators of Proper Focus on School's Mission	Rating
1. Defines mission of school and your role in its attainment.	5 4 3 2 1
2. Disseminates goals and purposes of schools to stakeholders.	5 4 3 2 1
3. Works individually and with other school leaders to influence state and federal education legislation.	5 4 3 2 1
4. Recommends the adoption of school board policy that assures proper educational focus.	5 4 3 2 1
5. Sets priorities that focus on most significant goals and tasks.	5 4 3 2 1
6. Takes a stand in opposition to pressure groups that push agendas not compatible with mission.	5 4 3 2 1
7. Involves stakeholders in developing the mission and goals of the school.	5 4 3 2 1
8. Conducts needs assessment to define strengths and developmental needs.	5 4 3 2 1
9. Contacts state and federal legislators concerning needs and limitations.	5 4 3 2 1
10. Uses comprehensive planning to focus on school mission.	5 4 3 2 1
11. Establishes criteria for determining program relevancy.	5 4 3 2 1

ON THE JOB DEVELOPMENT PLANS AND ACTIVITIES
(FOCUSING ON THE "TRUE" MISSION OF THE SCHOOL)

Instructions: The purpose of this chart is to provide you with a simple way for you to list your strengths and developmental needs, prioritize your improvement objectives, and list strategies that you might use to reach your goals. Reflect on past experiences and review all personal assessment data, including the previous page, to complete this task.

Strengths	Developmental Needs

Improvement Objectives	Possible Strategies

"BACK HOME" APPLICATIONS
(Focusing on the "True" Mission of the School)

Instructions: Based on your understanding of the lesson and the corollaries, pick one or two of the skills and consider your previous experiences and possible future applications "back home" in your leadership role.

SKILL	*PREVIOUS EXPERIENCE*	*FUTURE APPLICATIONS*
Can't Be All Things to All People,		
Clear and Consistent Themes,		
Getting to Closure Requires Processing,		
Being Pro-Active and Re-Active, and		
Using Existing Leadership/ Management Tools		

Lesson 9

KEEP IN MIND THAT ONE OF THE MOST EFFECTIVE WAYS TO LEARN AND GROW IS TO BENEFIT FROM YOUR CRITICAL PAST MISTAKES.

- Look back through reflection and analyze the conditions under which you made blunders and how you behaved in the situations. Also, analyze your successes and the successes of others. Recall the lessons you learned or could have learned from these past experiences. Incorporate this learning strategy as a tool for future learning.

UNDERSTANDING THE LESSON

Leaders learn from their mistakes. To succeed, leaders must acknowledge and understand past successes and failures and use this information to eliminate shortcomings. Emphasize that your staff, as well as you, need to learn from mistakes, not be afraid to take chances, conduct self-evaluations, and reflect on past experiences. One leader said it this way, "Successes help build self-confidence; failure gives you insight and assists you in paving new and better roads." Another said, "Anything that won't kill you outright is bound to make you stronger." Still another referred to John Dewey in talking about learning by doing, "I've concluded that you might learn more from your mistakes than your successes."

In addition to reflecting on past errors and then developing new ways of handling issues, our most effective leaders saw admitting that they had made a mistake and taking responsibility for the mistake as a sign of strength as rather than weakness. They analyze each situation to understand what they would do differently if they found themselves in similar situations in the future. They recognize that leaders who are trying to accomplish important undertakings will also make mistakes in the future. They advise that reflection on experiences should be used not only as a teaching tool for self, but for others within the organization. One leader was quick to point out that he tries not to obsess over making mistakes; he asks himself what is the worst thing that could happen.

Recognizing that the nature of the work of leadership is messy and full of ambiguity pulls leaders out of their comfort zones. Sometimes they have to let go of their initial plan to implement alternatives that were not their first choices. One piece of advice was for leaders to always ask themselves, "Is this the hill I want to die on?" They note that a confidant is necessary to help keep perspective and sanity.

Leaders who are new to their positions often make more mistakes than more experienced leaders. One extremely stressful leadership mistake is making commitments to more than one person at the same time. To implement damage control, an apology is always in order. Such an experience tends to make one more conscious of his or her decision-making processes. By practicing reflection on a daily basis, learning and growing as a leader is a natural occurrence.

In general, leaders recognize that making mistakes is a part of life and a part of leading. Their awareness of their own vulnerability is recognized when they become over extended and have their "plates full." They know when to revisit their obligations and then tend to focus on quality of activity and relationships rather than quantity. They know themselves, acknowledge their past successes and failures, and reflect on how their strengths and weaknesses affected the outcomes they produced.

NOTES:

_____

_____

_____

_____

UNDERSTANDING THE COROLLARIES

Corollary 1
Effective educational leaders play "what if" effectively, creating hypothetical responses for situations that may or may not happen to prepare when the stakes are high.

Playing "what if" is usually future oriented, but reflection on past events by this means is also useful to leaders. Leaders who can anticipate how various stakeholders might respond to a particular situation or set of circumstances will be more effective. "What if" scenarios are commonly used by leaders who consider themselves to be people watchers and who imagine how they might respond as leaders if they were an active part of the situation they are observing. Anticipating how a situation may unfold and how the players might react is a common practice for leaders who study virtually every phase of school operations. This is true at the building level, as well as at the district-level in such matters as preparation for board meetings and personnel appointments. A superintendent said, "I've discovered that playing 'what if' with my executive staff is one of the best ways to improve decision-making. It has virtually eliminated our making impulsive knee-jerk decisions." Superintendents point out, however, "frequent turnover of board presidents causes problems."

When leaders reflect on an event that has already occurred, they are extremely interested in understanding what caused the event to happen. They spend more energy in understanding causes than on what actually happened. Principals and district-level leaders then assess the damage. A district-level leader stated that, "In any given situation, ask yourself the question, 'On a Richter Scale of 1 to 10, what is this?' I find most things are a 2. Also, ask, 'What is the worst thing that can happen?'" Their advice for future challenges is to "carefully assess your situation, weighing all factors before making substantive change."

Using reflective writing, perhaps keeping a reflective learning journal, is a tool used by leaders to increase their skills at playing "what if." They play out questions around sticky situations involving parents, school employees, board issues, bond referenda, curriculum changes, discipline issues, and state and federal mandates. This approach increases their capacity for working with site-based management, as well as with special interest groups who often have opposing views.

Leaders are painfully aware of the implications of having to implement politically-imposed programs that may go against the philosophy of the school system. They tend to have a back-up plan, but sometimes find themselves doing very "unpleasant" things to help move them closer to the true goals for their organizations. One superintendent said, "One time I felt so strongly about an issue that I would do anything I had to do to address the problem short of doing something illegal, unethical, or immoral."

Effective leaders, over time, begin to realize that there are frequent unanticipated consequences that accompany the leadership process. In responding to these unanticipated consequences, leaders conduct self-evaluations of their perception of their own performance in such situations. Through this reflection on practice, leaders are nearly always able to improve their practice of leadership. Embedded in this approach is an honest attempt to seek feedback on their performance.

Leaders also become skilled in developing a sense of timing. They recognize when the time is right to go forward with a recommendation and when it is more important to hold off. However, in leading effectively, their mantra is to think ahead whenever possible.

NOTES:

_____

_____

_____

_____

Corollary 2
The successful educational leader may appear to think one way and act in another. Experience teaches a leader that the shortest distance between two points may be an indirect line. This can require using strategies that, to the untrained eye, may appear inconsistent and contradictory.

The requirements of leadership cause leaders to face in more than one direction at a time. An example shared by one leader, who happened to be a superintendent, was his position on providing leadership development for his principals and assistant principals and, at the same time, providing opportunities for teachers to become more effective in leading themselves through the process of teacher empowerment. Another superintendent of a district whose student population was in excess of 40 percent African-American lost his only African-American board member in the board election. He publicly stated his belief that it was inappropriate to have an all white board governing a district with a significant minority population; but, at the same time, he had to work with the board that he acquired. This was especially difficult since the majority of the board members failed to see that lack of African-American representation on the board was an issue.

One superintendent viewed the state department of public instruction in his state as another special interest group that had to be managed. Her district was a district of significant size with a well staffed central office, so the special support available from the state was not all that important. However, when the state superintendent of public instruction came to town for a visit, she rolled out the red carpet to ensure positive public relations with the state agency and with the state superintendent on a personal basis.

Superintendents, district-level leaders, and building-level leaders all wrestled with the issue of whether to increase or relax supervision of individuals and programs. What typically happens is that the decision to increase or decrease supervision is situational. Some programs and some individuals may need more supervision than others. A deputy superintendent in a large urban district said, "We have had to move away from the idea that one size fits all. Some people and some programs simply require more supervision than others."

This idea of thinking and acting in contradictions creates an environment where things are viewed and often experienced on multiple levels. Leaders must develop the skills to understand how things work on multiple levels and convey this information, when appropriate, to stakeholder groups. Leaders who are able to reframe and rethink events in a new way can often develop a new understanding. However, one of the deeper contradictions that leaders face involves the tensions that exist between actions that are professionally desirable and actions that the public finds desirable. One implication of these tensions is that superintendents frequently act in ways that keep options open and provide for a variety of alternatives that may be considered in issue resolution.

Active leaders who are making important decisions will make their share of mistakes. A fact that is commonly held among leaders is that, through reflection on their mistakes, they can acquire important knowledge. This is common practice at the district level and at the building level. Leaders use the information that they glean from reflecting on their mistakes to refrain from making the same mistake in the future.

School principals note that sharing information with others is helpful in making one more effective, but there is a need to exercise care in choosing when and how to share the information. Principals believe that people, in general, are resistant to change and providing too much information too quickly can generate a stressful environment for their staffs. Planting "seeds of information," trusting one's instincts, and not being in a hurry to rush to closure are methods that work for many principals. A general guide is to follow your instincts, "but pray they will always be in the interests of students."

Finally, be aware that there are leader watchers who are paying attention to how you act at all times. They will be especially interested in how you read the culture of your organization and how you respond to both the positive and negative aspects. Our experienced leaders advise, "Choose your battles carefully. The ultimate goal is to 'win the war.'" Take great care in surrounding yourself with people you trust.

NOTES:

_____

_____

_____

_____

Corollary 3
The successful educational leader can learn far more from his/her past mistakes by discussing his/her mishaps with other leaders who have had similar bad experiences.

Remember that you are not in the school leadership business alone. For every good and bad experience you have had, there are hundreds, if not thousands of others, who have encountered similar kinds of challenges. Learn from them and their experiences. Talk with other leaders on a one-to-one basis rather than reacting in frustration. Continue to rethink and to think ahead. Keeping multiple balls in the air is a part of leading; but, when possible, complete as much of each job as you can before moving on to another. Don't hesitate to admit it when you have made a mistake.

Superintendents recommend that, when you accept a new position, try to be very tactful in learning about the perceived mistakes made by your predecessors. A superintendent stated, "When I moved into a new superintendency, people were eager to point out the mistakes my predecessors had made. To my surprise, in my previous job, I had made the same errors." Another leader suggests, "Let sleeping dogs lie. When you have no good reasons for doing something, you have one good reason for forgetting it."

NOTES:

_____

_____

_____

_____

**ASSESSMENT INSTRUMENT TO DETERMINE THE EXTENT
THAT YOU CURRENTLY OR HAVE IMPROVED IN LEARNING FROM PAST
EXPERIENCES OR BENEFITING FROM CRITICAL MISTAKES**

Instructions: This instrument is designed to help you determine your current status and change in status relative to benefiting from critical mistakes. Before reacting to the scale, decide whether you wish to appraise your current practices or the changes you have made in these practices over a particular period of time.

Current Status	*Rating*	*Change In Status*
Uses to <u>very great</u> extent	5	Made <u>significant</u> positive change
Uses to <u>great</u> extent	4	Made <u>some</u> positive change
Uses to <u>moderate</u> extent	3	Made <u>little or no</u> change
Uses to <u>a little</u> extent	2	Made <u>some</u> negative change
Uses to <u>no</u> extent	1	Made <u>significant</u> negative change

Indicators of Learning from Past Mistakes	Rating
1. Learns from past mistakes.	5 4 3 2 1
2. Plays "what if" effectively to avoid mistakes.	5 4 3 2 1
3. Anticipates problems and takes corrective actions.	5 4 3 2 1
4. Learns from predecessor's mistakes.	5 4 3 2 1
5. Knows the importance of timing when making change.	5 4 3 2 1
6. Acts on impulse when necessary, but always in the best interest of students.	5 4 3 2 1
7. Knows how to deal with contradictions.	5 4 3 2 1
8. Learns from other superintendents who have faced similar problems.	5 4 3 2 1
9. Is tolerant of others who make mistakes.	5 4 3 2 1
10. Encourages staff to take risks and learn from both successes and mistakes.	5 4 3 2 1
11. Advises board relative to the positive and negative consequences of decisions.	5 4 3 2 1
12. Provides training to staff that emphasizes learning from mistakes.	5 4 3 2 1

ON THE JOB DEVELOPMENT PLANS AND ACTIVITIES
(BENEFITS FROM CRITICAL PAST MISTAKES)

Instructions: The purpose of this chart is to provide you with a simple way for you to list your strengths and developmental needs, prioritize your improvement objectives, and list strategies that you might use to reach your goals. Reflect on past experiences and review all personal assessment data, including the previous page, to complete this task.

Strengths	Developmental Needs
Improvement Objectives	**Possible Strategies**

"BACK HOME" APPLICATIONS
(Benefits from Critical Past Mistakes)

Instructions: Based on your understanding of the lesson and the corollaries, pick one or two of the skills and consider your previous experiences and possible future applications "back home" in your leadership role.

SKILL	PREVIOUS EXPERIENCE	FUTURE APPLICATIONS
Learn from Past Mistakes,		
Play "What If,"		
Utilize Strategies That Appear Contradictory, and		
Share Negative Experiences With Others		

Lesson 10

SINCE COLLEAGUES ARE PROBABLY EXPERIENCING OR HAVE EXPERIENCED DIFFICULTIES SIMILAR TO THOSE YOU ARE NOW FACING, NETWORKING AND USING MENTORS ARE EFFECTIVE WAYS TO HELP SOLVE PROBLEMS.

- Develop and use a network of reliable colleagues with whom you can exchange ideas, information, strategies, and nurturing.

UNDERSTANDING THE LESSON

To become effective in positions of authority, leaders must become perpetual learners. Leaders at all levels within school organizations can learn more and more by talking with other leaders; reading about current innovations and the newest thinking in their field, attending professional conferences at the local, state, and national levels; and networking. Talking with colleagues and networking with others who face similar challenges can prove to be especially important if you can establish relationships that allow for truly honest exchanges and feedback. Join professional organizations, seek out trusted colleagues, and take time to just sit and talk. Seeking the advice of veteran leaders, as well as serving as a mentor to developing leaders produces a mutual benefit and will lead to more effective problem solving. One leader pointed out the personal benefits of serving as a coach for a developing leader in another school district when she said, "Coaching another person in a different district may be more enjoyable because of the lack of tension in working together."

A priority approach used by many leaders is to get to know administrators from other states while attending national conventions. This approach has resulted in finding both formal and informal mentors. "Networking with fellow central office personnel has become one of the best leadership enhancing strategies," is a sentiment expressed by a district-level leader and echoed by many others. It is interesting to note that the emphasis is often on seeking assistance with problems that may occur in the future. At the same time leaders are frequently consumed with the problems of the day. One leader said it this way, "Lately the state and feds are mandating new programs so fast that it is difficult to implement what is intended. I use networking to obtain answers; and, when my colleagues are also in the dark, I at least know that I'm not alone."

The more you learn as a leader the more you are capable of learning. This increased knowledge will make you more effective. Work extremely hard at developing a network of people that you can trust to give you good advice on difficult challenges. Continue positive communications within your own work environment. Ask questions and learn from past successes and mistakes of your own, as well as those of others.

NOTES:

_____

_____

_____

_____

UNDERSTANDING THE COROLLARIES

Corollary 1
Effective educational leaders not only take advantage of mentors to learn and grow, they use this vital training technique to improve the performance of all of the district's employees.

Mentoring is especially effective in introducing new workers to their job responsibilities. One important key to successful mentoring is matching the mentor with the learner and seeking compatibility in personality traits and professional interests. A middle-level educational leader said it this way, "When I took my first administrative position, I learned more from my mentor than I did from all of my college and university courses in school administration." To illustrate the importance of being sure that mentors and mentees are compatible, we can look at the comment from a mentorship experience that was negative. The leader said, "I had a serious personality conflict with my first mentor. The entire experience was a total fiasco." Frequently, when the match is good, a by-product of mentorship is that the mentor learns just as much or more than the person being mentored.

Practicing leaders comment on the importance of recruiting teachers who have leadership potential and then helping them develop their potential. The prevailing attitude among leaders who incorporate this idea into their job descriptions is that the potential retirement of so many administrators creates a great need to develop teachers to become lead teachers, assistant principals, and principals in the coming years. Some leaders actually formalize the recruitment of teachers who are deemed to possess leadership potential as a part of their career goal setting. One leaders who spends considerable time in recruitment said, "I know that leaders are made not born, but I look for natural leadership when I am recruiting."

Mentoring is an important trust building activity between the mentor and mentee. Mentors see their involvement with developing leaders as opportunities to "bounce ideas back and forth." Those who have been mentored, over time, become a part of a network of professional associates.

A principal noted that she was pleased to serve in the capacity of mentor and coach for her staff. In describing her experiences, she said, "This is a wonderful experience and an awesome challenge at times. It is good to network with other colleagues and to give, as well as receive assistance. We often do this to help our staff. We also have received extensive training on mentoring and coaching."

Leaders see ways that they might modify their mentoring experiences in the future. For example, although there is overwhelming support among practicing leaders for ongoing mentoring and coaching, some indicate that they would increase the amount of professional development made available to their staffs. They see this as an indication that they feel their staffs are valued enough to employ consultants and staff development specialists to provide professional training. They believe that their staffs need to be better prepared to participate in the decision-making process and that, as formal leaders, they also need to work on increased delegation of duties as opposed to trying to do too many things themselves. They saw a need to delegate beyond their immediate assistants.

An entry-level administrator captured the importance of a mentor in his development when he said:

> So far in my career, I have sought a mentor to guide my educational career choices. Especially when I was a high school teacher, my principal was a major influence on my pursuit of my MSA. He appointed me as assistant principal in the school. Having a mentor has been very beneficial to my career as a young administrator.

A mid-career principal stated:

> I have found it very helpful to call upon others who have had similar experiences or who serve in the same capacity which I do. Usually another set of ears and a previous similar encounter by the colleague help me come to an answer or resolution and make me realize the fluid nature of a crisis or problem. The principalship is a lonely job and it's important to have colleagues, friends, and mentors whom I can trust.

NOTES:

_____

_____

_____

_____

Corollary 2
An effective, but rarely used training technique, is a personnel exchange program.

When there is a critical job function that needs to be performed in your schools and there is no one on your current staff to fit the bill, consider exchanging personnel with another district that has faced similar challenges. This technique will not only give you time to train a current worker to do the job, but it will save you money. An efficiently operated exchange program is one of the most cost-effective ways to provide critical training and to obtain new ideas. One comment captured the idea this way:

> Way back in time when there was an abundance of federal education money, I was fortunate enough to have been involved in an exchange program. I have never had a more profitable experience. Since then, I have talked a neighboring superintendent into sharing personnel. He loves it too.

NOTES:

_____

_____

_____

_____

Corollary 3
Formal and informal networking is an excellent strategy for helping insure that educational leaders interpret and implement state/federal mandates correctly.

Many of the deadlines for implementing some of the federal and state-mandated programs are so restrictive that it is virtually impossible for school-based personnel to interpret and implement the legislation correctly. Networking can begin to address the problem. An effective strategy is to create ad hoc networking groups to obtain ideas and recommendations from many sources. Have a group of colleagues come together regularly to discuss events and concerns. A local superintendent said it this way, "Tis true that 'misery loves company,' but I prefer to be happy with my friends. For this reason, I join forces with my colleagues to solve problems."

NOTES:

_____

_____

_____

_____

Corollary 4
The effective educational leader not only uses networking to solve problems, he/she employs this strategy to prevent problems.

Collectively and individually school leaders need to be proactive rather than reactive in determining new educational initiatives and policies. National, state, and local educational organizations, as well as informal groups of school employees should join together to shape the future of education. Too many school leaders strive to become proficient in damage control when they should devote their time to assuring that the damage never occurs. Politicians who often know little about education make far more critical decisions about what goes on in the schools than teachers and administrators. Educators need to join together to reverse this trend. An elementary school principal expressed it this way when she said, "Whoever said an ounce of prevention is worth a pound of cure must have been thinking about the weighty problems in the schools." Our leaders give the advice that educational leaders need to develop relationships with others in similar positions and confer with them regularly.

A district-level leader new to her position in a large metropolitan school district noted that she had not found a lot of people in her specialty area with whom she could net work. In her previous position in a smaller district and in a different role, she indicated that she "had developed an extensive network of 'buddies' to talk with and discuss questions and concerns." She mentioned how she really misses this and captured her thoughts this way, "I don't think I realized how much I enjoyed being able to just call and talk with someone who was experiencing the same problems and restraints." She went on to say:

> Because I truly miss the interactions and fun learning times with others, I plan to attend a magnet school conference this summer. Hopefully, I will meet people from across the nation who deal daily with magnet school issues from whom I can learn and exchange ideas. I see now that I will always need others to support me and just be around to answer questions, give advice, laugh and cry with, and act as sounding boards for new ideas.

NOTES:

_____

_____

_____

ASSESSMENT INSTRUMENT TO DETERMINE THE EXTENT THAT YOU CURRENTLY OR HAVE IMPROVED IN MENTORING AND NETWORKING

Instructions: This instrument is designed to help you determine your current status and change in status relative to mentoring and networking. Before reacting to the scale, decide whether you wish to appraise your current practices or the changes you have made in these practices over a particular period of time.

Current Status	*Rating*	*Change In Status*
Uses to <u>very great</u> extent	5	Made <u>significant</u> positive change
Uses to <u>great</u> extent	4	Made <u>some</u> positive change
Uses to <u>moderate</u> extent	3	Made <u>little or no</u> change
Uses to <u>a little</u> extent	2	Made <u>some</u> negative change
Uses to <u>no</u> extent	1	Made <u>significant</u> negative change

Indicators of Effective Networking/Mentoring	Rating				
1. Develops and uses a network of colleagues to solve problems.	5	4	3	2	1
2. Attends state and local training programs.	5	4	3	2	1
3. Uses mentors to improve own and staffs' skills.	5	4	3	2	1
4. Employs personnel exchange programs with other districts.	5	4	3	2	1
5. Uses networking to help interpret and implement new mandated state and federal initiatives.	5	4	3	2	1
6. Encourages inter-district ad hoc networking to solve critical "and interim" problems.	5	4	3	2	1
7. Uses networking to prevent, as well as solve problems.	5	4	3	2	1
8. Serves as mentor for inexperienced leaders.	5	4	3	2	1
9. Joins colleagues in lobbying for relevant education reform.	5	4	3	2	1
10. Provides mentoring services for new teachers.	5	4	3	2	1
11. Keeps up-to-date on nationwide exemplary instructional and administrative programs.	5	4	3	2	1
12. Recognizes and celebrates outstanding mentoring on the part of staff.	5	4	3	2	1

ON THE JOB DEVELOPMENT PLANS AND ACTIVITIES
(NETWORKING AND MENTORING)

Instructions: The purpose of this chart is to provide you with a simple way for you to list your strengths and developmental needs, prioritize your improvement objectives, and list strategies that you might use to reach your goals. Reflect on past experiences and review all personal assessment data, including the previous page, to complete this task.

Strengths	Developmental Needs
Improvement Objectives	**Possible Strategies**

"BACK HOME" APPLICATIONS
(Networking and Mentoring)

Instructions: Based on your understanding of the lesson and the corollaries, pick one or two of the skills and consider your previous experiences and possible future applications "back home" in your leadership role.

SKILL	PREVIOUS EXPERIENCE	FUTURE APPLICATIONS
Networking and Mentoring, **Personnel Exchange, and** **Interpreting State/Federal Mandates**		

Lesson 11

IN MAKING CHANGES THAT IMPACT ON THE SCHOOL ORGANIZATION, INVOLVE REPRESENTATIVE INTERESTED PARTIES IN ANALYZING RELEVANT DATA AND DEVELOPING GOALS AND STRATEGIES. DISSEMINATE YOUR PLANS AND IMPLEMENTATION RESULTS TO ALL STAKEHOLDERS.

• Establish and follow a systematic procedure for implementing changes.

UNDERSTANDING THE LESSON

It should be a commonly understood fact among leaders that the people who are expected to implement change should be involved in identifying and designing what the change will look like. Too many leaders make the mistake of believing that a top down change mandate will be automatically implemented. Even when it appears that the change is being implemented, it is usually a response that is more a temporary compliance than a real commitment.

One experienced principal said it this way:

> I have learned from various leadership roles that, if people are not involved in decision-making and do not have access to information from the beginning, it is very hard to get them committed to an idea. Also, when and how information is shared is essential. An example is the reaction of my sixth grade teachers to the notion of a four-teacher team when I gained a teaching position after the first ten days of school this year. When I first approached them, they were very adamant that it wouldn't work. I offered them the alternative of two two-teacher teams and I gave them the flexibility to come up with a schedule and teaching assignments for either two or four. They liked the idea and they came up with a plan for a four-teacher team that worked.

In making changes, our leaders recommend that it is important to develop a sense of priorities and a schedule for implementation of the change that allows time for addressing issues revised by those who are expected to implement the change. Be mindful of change readiness issues in general and the climate for change overall. A common theme that resonates with our leaders includes the importance of effective communication at all stages of the change process as a way of creating buy-in and maintaining support and ownership. The importance of using data effectively as a driving force for change is an emerging theme and one that is viewed to be an equalizing force for the leader in charge. In a sense, when the leader has done her homework, she becomes the expert on what the data say and then data can be used to promote the need for change. Of course, the primary leadership activity is the ability to oversee the whole change process in a way that the change becomes institutionalized.

Leaders at various levels throughout the school organization believe that their leadership teams must have "lots of ownership" when it comes to decision-making. In using a team approach, the leader must have a strong understanding of what each team member's strengths are and what the overall team profile is like. In other words, as a team, what are the true strengths of the team and where are the gaps that will interfere with optimum performance. This allows the formal leader to better understand what can be completely delegated, what can be delegated and then monitored, and what must be addressed directly by the leader herself. These types of understanding help the leader see where intervention strategies need to be introduced to provide both individual and team development.

NOTES:

_____

_____

_____

_____

UNDERSTANDING THE COROLLARIES

Corollary 1
Timing is an essential tool.

Timing is a key in many areas of life and is certainly critical in implementing change. This includes knowing which battles to fight, when to introduce a change, when to wait, when to turn loose, and when to retire. Do not procrastinate when unpleasant tasks have to be addressed. A district-level leader captured it this way, "Timing can or will determine who you will become in an organizational sense, what your job might be, the successes that you realize from your job, and the speed in which you move up the hierarchy." A principal went on to say, "Timing events is critical, especially when dealing with teachers. An untimely change can be short lived if the timing is not perfect. Morale, time of the week, time of the day, and many other variables can affect how people react to news or decisions." Other examples involving building-based leadership include considerations about knowing when to introduce something new, either at a staff meeting or during a planning period, and when to postpone a special event in order to avoid "disrupting the entire day."

When it comes to knowing which battles to fight, leaders feel that generally you should not put up an excessive battle on an issue that you know will lose from the outset. One example shared by a high school principal has to do with the reconfiguration of a softball field in order to open up more space for the football press box. He said, "Shortly after presenting this idea to our central office, it became evident that the opposition had the upper hand. Even though several members of our coaching staff really wanted the change, I decided to retire from the arena." When it comes to a standard operating procedure, one superintendent talked about his approach, "I have begun to abide by the Serenity Prayer. I have learned to change the things I can, accept the things I cannot, and have the wisdom to know the difference."

When leaders have a strong personal need to complete major change initiatives quickly and construct an agenda to do so, the outcomes of such an approach can be undesirable. Many "impatient" leaders find that the approach of being too direct and "getting straight to the facts" can be detrimental. By understanding the law of timing, leaders can improve their capacity for leading change by making adjustments as needed. This requires strong skills in reading situations and people. An elected superintendent discussed his experiences with leadership:

Just as a rudder is to a ship, so is leadership to a school district. Providing that leadership in an effective manner is a complicated process at best, but even more complex when tied to the position of elected superintendent. Legislative mandates, contract stipulations, and legal requirements can easily become political issues. These issues, without constant vigilance, can impact on your ability to reach important goals.

An elementary principal, new to her school but not inexperienced as a principal, ran head long into a faculty and staff who wanted to maintain the status quo. Her perspective was, "The school did not want a 'responsible discipline' program so I held off trying to sell them on it for one year." Her experience, like that of many other leaders, is that you need to build some nucleus of support before moving forward with unpopular initiatives.

NOTES:

_____

_____

_____

_____

_____

Corollary 2
To avoid confusing and overwhelming your staff and to help ensure success, new programs should be implemented and tested on a pilot basis.

Field testing prior to full implementation is a cost-effective and non-threatening way to bring about improvement. Full formative (process) and summative (outcome) evaluations should be planned and conducted on all innovative efforts. Information gleaned from these evaluations should be used to make corrections or abandon the new effort. Successful procedures may be replicated. However, past success does not always guarantee future program funding. Referring to implementing new programs, a district-level leader stated:

> One of the best programs that was ever funded with federal money was the Title III or Innovative Programs. It required the submission of a comprehensive plan and implementation under tight controls. Unfortunately, when the feds did not fund the program anymore, it was not adopted by local and state governments.

Those leaders who consider themselves to be strong instructional leaders believe that "there will always be change" and their previous experiences with leading instructional changes will determine how they approach future instructional projects. Instructional leaders see the benefit of "small doses and help with follow-up" to understand what should be done to increase the possibility of a smooth transition. An instructional leader at the district-level captured her experience after attending a national conference:

> My most recent experience was a visit to Chicago to a national conference on change implementation. I wanted to come back and quickly change the mindset of resistors. I learned this does not work. Change should be done in small increments and not delegated, but just shared in the initial phase. There is a need for flexibility and compromise.

NOTES:

_____

_____

_____

_____

Corollary 3
The successful educational leader improvises. He/she develops capacity in using resources and ideas in a complex environment that is full of unanticipated consequences.

For educational leaders in today's environment, change is the only constant that they will face. In attempting to lead change in school organizations, it is frequently impossible to predict the exact nature of the irrational behavior that leaders may encounter. Therefore, leaders must use dexterity in learning to think on their feet. Remaining calm under extremely stressful circumstances is an absolute. Developing the ability to use this strategy will allow for improvising or adapting one's approach on either a moment's notice or over a longer timeframe. A district-level leader stated, "Improvisation is the ability to use the strengths of all facets of society to better our schools."

Responding superintendents employ a number of improvisation strategies when facing difficult leadership challenges. Examples of challenges that required strong leadership and improvisation included having one's effectiveness judged on the basis of "turning around middle schools," quickly increasing Scholastic Aptitude Test results, advancing a student redistricting plan, losing the only African-American board member in a district that had a significant African-American student population, and discovering improprieties in the exceptional children's program when the program was led by a 40-year veteran who was also the brother of the board chairman.

Improvisation strategies employed by superintendents to address these challenges covered a wide range of approaches. To assist with "turning the middle schools around," the superintendent turned to a major corporation located in the city and asked that they sponsor after-school academies that offered free tutoring to all students who wished to receive the services. The corporate sponsor paid teachers for working after school and incurred the additional costs for providing bus transportation for students in the after-school program.

When it came to raising SAT scores, the superintendent quickly implemented SAT preparation courses at each high school in the district. Students could take these courses free of charge after school and on a volunteer basis. The result of this effort, in part, was a significant and fast increase in scores. The superintendent realized that this was an "artificial" increase, but it bought her enough time to engineer curriculum changes that, over time, would get more students in higher-level courses much earlier in their high school careers.

The redistricting challenge was an issue due to a division on the board, with one faction wanting to resegregate the schools and one faction wanting to maintain an integrated school system reflective of the racial make-up of the community. The superintendent was a strong proponent of maintaining racially-integrated schools and put together a cross-functional team consisting of a curriculum expert, a facilities expert, a transportation expert, and a legal advisor. The superintendent remained active in the project, but, at a distance made sure that plan after plan was presented over a two year time span that protected the integrity of integrated schools. He knew that the board would "discuss each plan to death" and that public hearings would take "forever." In the end, however, the superintendent left the district and a new majority board surfaced and implemented an assignment plan that left many schools terrifically underutilized and racially identifiable.

When one school system lost its only African-American board member, the superintendent moved quickly to assemble a group of representative African-Americans to serve in an informal advisory capacity to the superintendent. This approach, although unpopular with some board members, was a symbolic act by the superintendent that demonstrated his commitment to all students in the district. This approach served as an answer to a difficult situation until the next board election when two African-Americans were elected to serve on the board of education.

One major impropriety encountered by a superintendent in a large district in the south was a grossly mismanaged exceptional children's program. Program improprieties consisted of everything from intentional non-compliance to the use of school-owned equipment for personal purposes. To make matters worse, the director of the program was also the brother of the board chair. The superintendent quietly contacted the state department of public instruction and requested that the state conduct a complete program audit, but made it appear, with the support of the state department, that the state had initiated the audit. Within a few months, the director had retired, a new director was employed, and the exceptional children's program was on the road to recovery.

One of the more dramatic examples shared by a superintendent was his finding that there were as many as five "tracks" in the high schools, as well as a huge number of course offerings, many of which were obsolete. The superintendent, with the help of his high school director and the director's staff, determined that it would take a student over 30 years to take all of the courses typically offered in any one high school. Many of the obsolete courses were taught by senior faculty who had managed to retain employment even though their enrollments were extremely low. The expense of offering courses for which very few students enrolled was exorbitant. This, along with resegregation within the school as a result of the tracking, prompted the superintendent to employ the services of an outside group to conduct a curriculum audit. The audit results, although initially resented by some board members and some "elitists," became a high leverage tool for eliminating a large number of courses and reducing the number of tracks at the high school level. The superintendent, in commenting on this situation, said:

> Be flexible and compromise when you can, but never compromise your basic values. Keep a sense of humor and laugh at your self and others. Don't hesitate to use outside sources to help advance your agenda, especially when your agenda has the interest of students at its core.

Regarding improvisation at the middle school level, a middle school principal said:

> Involve the stakeholders and create buy-in from the start when promoting an agenda or creating change. Pay attention to details and people's agendas. Listen and provide direction for where you want to go. Keep in mind that when making systematic changes, one must manage vision and purpose and communicate this. Additionally important for this circumstance of change is the need for effective teams, conflict management, and innovation. Create changes by engaging groups that previously have not felt empowered. Make improvisational changes when necessary to get quick outcomes that prove the point.

NOTES:

_____

_____

_____

_____

Corollary 4
The first critical step in making improvements and bringing about desirable educational reform is to conduct a comprehensive needs assessment.

All representative players should be involved in determining the type of data to be collected and analyzed, the sources for securing the needed information, and how the data will be used. Possible information sources can include information about students, parents, staff, other stakeholder groups, and the availability of resources. Leaders believe that the most relevant data for planning improvements include information about student and staff potential for improvement of performance, along with the opinions and attitudes of various stakeholders. Leaders advise, "You're inviting trouble if you don't consider the needs and interests of your board members." Another leader suggests that, "Educators frequently make decisions without analyzing the information they have on hand. This is even worse than ignoring facts before your troops go to battle."

NOTES:

_____

_____

_____

_____

Corollary 5
Comprehensive school improvement planning is a vital management tool that provides direction and ensures accountability.

It is not uncommon to find several planning documents that have been produced to provide direction for either a school district or individual schools. The challenge is that rarely do the plans get off the shelf and rarely does anyone in a position of authority work to consolidate the plans into a user-friendly single planning document. Too many plans illicit the response that we will just "keep doing our thing;" because, before we can get anything implemented, someone will "lay another plan on us." Effective leaders quickly recognize the importance of consolidating all planning efforts into a single, more manageable document that contains the vision, mission, beliefs, major focus areas for improvement, goals, improvement strategies, role responsibilities, implementation timelines, and evaluation procedures. This approach is the first step in beginning to assure true teamwork and cooperation. A principal in a small school with limited staff said, "We simply do not have the human resources to keep up with all that is mandated. We do what we can and the rest falls through the cracks."

The planning process is an excellent technique for encouraging involvement of stakeholders with varied interests. A seasoned principal recalled his first year as a principal, "Whoever first said, 'If you fail to plan, you plan to fail,' didn't fail to make the point with me. In my first year as a principal, I didn't have a plan, and I paid the price."

NOTES:

_____

_____

_____

_____

ASSESSMENT INSTRUMENT TO DETERMINE THE EXTENT THAT YOU CURRENTLY EMPLOY OR HAVE IMPROVED IN ANALYZING RELEVANT DATA AND DEVELOPING GOALS AND STRATEGIES

Instructions: This instrument is designed to help you determine your current status and change in status relative to analyzing relevant data and developing goals and strategies. Before reacting to the scale, decide whether you wish to appraise your current practices or the changes you have made in these practices over a particular period of time.

Current Status	*Rating*	*Change In Status*
Uses to <u>very great</u> extent	5	Made <u>significant</u> positive change
Uses to <u>great</u> extent	4	Made <u>some</u> positive change
Uses to <u>moderate</u> extent	3	Made <u>little or no</u> change
Uses to <u>a little</u> extent	2	Made <u>some</u> negative change
Uses to <u>no</u> extent	1	Made <u>significant</u> negative change

Indicators of Involvement in Collecting and Analyzing Data	**Rating**				
1. Maintains comprehensive database for planning and decision making.	5	4	3	2	1
2. Conducts timely needs assessment that obtains input from staff and stakeholders.	5	4	3	2	1
3. Shares/disseminates pertinent information with interested parties.	5	4	3	2	1
4. Knows when and how to make change.	5	4	3	2	1
5. Implements major change on a pilot basis and then evaluates and adapts or abandons.	5	4	3	2	1
6. Involves key educational players in developing and implementing improvement plans.	5	4	3	2	1
7. Encourages staff to take calculated risks.	5	4	3	2	1
8. Requires that all new innovations be evaluated.	5	4	3	2	1
9. Provides training in managing change.	5	4	3	2	1
10. Seeks to find ways that the schools can be changed/improved.	5	4	3	2	1
11. Recognizes and celebrates successful innovation.	5	4	3	2	1
12. Has standards for ensuring the confidentiality of personal and sensitive information.	5	4	3	2	1

ON THE JOB DEVELOPMENT PLANS AND ACTIVITIES
(ANALYZING RELEVANT DATA AND DEVELOPING
GOALS AND STRATEGIES)

Instructions: The purpose of this chart is to provide you with a simple way for you to list your strengths and developmental needs, prioritize your improvement objectives, and list strategies that you might use to reach your goals. Reflect on past experiences and review all assessment data, including the previous page, to complete this task.

Strengths	Developmental Needs
Improvement Objectives	**Possible Strategies**

"BACK HOME" APPLICATIONS
(Analyzing Relevant Data and Developing Goals and Strategies)

Instructions: Based on your understanding of the lesson and the corollaries, pick one or two of the skills and consider your previous experiences and possible future applications "back home" in your leadership role.

SKILL	PREVIOUS EXPERIENCE	FUTURE APPLICATIONS
Involving Parties in Analyzing Data and Disseminating Results, **Timing,** **Piloting,** **Improvising, and** **Planning**		

Lesson 12

REMEMBER, THERE IS ONE "BOTTOM-LINE" CRITERION FOR MAKING EDUCATIONAL DECISIONS: WHAT EFFECT WILL THE DECISION HAVE ON THE WELFARE OF STUDENTS?

- Incorporate the "student interest" variable in making all major decisions for your school district.

UNDERSTANDING THE LESSON

This lesson is the lesson that is the heart of leadership for schools. Our leaders recognize that way too many decisions are determined by what is politically correct and are frequently so far removed from the student interest variable that they often border on ridiculous. There are many reasons for this, but a few include the lobbying power of special interest groups, the agenda of individual board members, and the power of those who control the dollars. Our leaders recommend that, when faced with difficult and often controversial challenges, it is extremely helpful to reframe the situation in terms of the student interest variable by asking what is in the best interest of students. Remembering the purpose of schools and constantly reminding yourself that education is "the key to opening doors for young people" will help you determine your best course of action. Those who are pushing their agenda for a different reason can sometimes be reined in if the leader raises the issue of how the decision will impact on students. A local superintendent said it this way, "When you want to initiate new programs, be prepared to show how this will positively affect our students' ability to learn and anticipate how others might try to stop your ideas by showing harm to students' ability to learn."

The importance of working with families of different cultural backgrounds to help create mutual understanding of school rules and expectations is noted by our leaders, especially those in leadership roles at the building level. This includes organizing special programs designed to recognize student achievement. This captures a visible demonstration of what leaders and their schools truly value in terms of student successes.

A district leader in a large metropolitan school district discussed a particularly challenging set of circumstances surrounding one of the schools under her direction.

> Teachers were fired, administrators were moved around, and a whole new staff had to undergo interviews to be hired. All of this was front page news for many weeks, so naturally the school system got a bad name. We

tried to change the image and introduce people to the 'new' school. One of our ploys was to purchase a large number of laptop computers for students and their families that could be taken home. The plan also included free internet access. This became a win-win situation for students and their families and the school got back its good reputation.

NOTES:

_____

_____

_____

_____

UNDERSTANDING THE COROLLARIES

Corollary 1
The successful educational leader must dramatize important issues and events to communicate his/her point of view. He/she must also be alert to seizing unanticipated opportunities for dramatization.

The demands on leaders and the sheer expectation that they be at practically any and all school and district events is a phenomenon that is difficult to explain unless you have experienced the time requirements of leadership. I can remember hearing stories of a school superintendent who assumed the superintendency of a very large district. The story says that the superintendent, upon assuming this new assignment, went over 40 days, including weekends, without eating a meal at home. This may be hard to believe if you have never been there. However, the demands on a superintendent for appearances both inside and outside the district, especially when first going to a new district, can be unbelievable. As one of my former associates used to say, "They just want to touch your garment." The interpretation is that those whom you are leading just want to see their superintendent up close and personal.

Think about the demands that are placed on high school principals and their assistants to be in attendance at school-sponsored events and activities after the "regular" workday. The expectation that administrators attend athletic contests; band, orchestra, and choral performances; drama club presentations; and every other form of extra-curricular activity imaginable usually translates to about four to five evenings a week with workdays in the 15- to 16-hour range.

Not only are administrators expected to attend such events, they are expected to "put their best foot forward." The question becomes how can leaders be "everything to everybody." The answer to this important challenge is to master the art of using drama through symbols and symbolic leadership behavior. Effective leaders have a flair for drama and are skilled at using symbols to convey to their constituents what is important.

One of my favorite true stories is a story about a school superintendent who discovered, during the early months of his tenure in a new assignment, that it had been almost a dozen years since the entire faculty of the district had come together for an opening of school convocation. The superintendent had assumed his new role during the middle of the year and had spent the first six months getting to know the district through school visits, speeches to civic clubs, and meetings with board members, parents, and members of the business community. During this first six months, in his judgment, the local newspapers had treated him fairly; but, in his mind, there was something missing. He wondered how

129

he could convey to the masses what he really considered to be important when it came to the schools. He felt that holding an opening convocation for the faculty would symbolically address some of his concerns, especially if he could get his message "right" At the same time, he pondered up until the morning of the convocation just what he could do to send the message about what he truly valued as their formal leader.

As the day of the convocation arrived, the superintendent had prepared his "let's put 'em to sleep speech 101." However, about two hours before the convocation, a light went off and he decided to use his five-year-old daughter, who was a rising kindergartner at the time, as a part of his presentation. So, at the conclusion of his speech, with over a thousand teachers in attendance and his board sitting on stage with him, he proceeded to introduce his daughter to the audience. He said, "On Monday, 17,000 students are going to walk through your doors and I want to introduce one of them." When his daughter walked out on stage, he continued, "This is Allison, my daughter. Now all of your students are not going to be like Allison. Not all of them are going to have the love that Allison has at home. In fact, some of them are going to be rich and some of them are going to be poor. Some of them will gifted; some will be handicapped; some will be dirty and need a bath. But all of them, like Allison, will need your love. So, love them first and then teach them."

What followed was an emotional scene with many tearful eyes in the audience and among some pretty hardcore board members. The superintendent had successfully, through having a flair for drama and using his daughter as a symbol for all students in the district, demonstrated what he truly valued as the formal leader in the district. This story was told by those in attendance for many years and had a powerful impact on the district and how the superintendent was perceived by the rank and file.

Our effective leaders have grown to understand that symbolism and symbolic gestures can be used to achieve desired outcomes. Due to the time demands placed on leaders, they must always search for high-leverage activities, through the use of drama and symbols, that will enable them to impart to all those looking on what they value and what they consider to be important. Leaders at many levels within school systems employ such approaches as recognizing student achievements through celebrations; recognition of student, faculty, and staff accomplishments at board meetings; sending out press releases on district accomplishments; conducting science and career fairs; and recognizing a teacher of the year. School principals use the concept of the "Honor Wall" in the front lobbies of their schools that highlight positive accomplishments of their "school families." There appears to be little substitute for the power of a personal congratulatory handwritten note. In fact, a former administrator ran into one of his former teachers in an airport. She proceeded to reach in her purse and display a handwritten note that he had written to her over fifteen years before. Develop a flair for drama and learn to use symbols and symbolic behavior to increase your effectiveness.

NOTES:

Corollary 2
All decisions and actions made or taken by the board of education and the administration must be consistent with the best interest of students.

An effective way for ensuring that policies and administrative decisions and actions are student centered is to formulate and adopt "zero tolerance" procedures that spell out actions related to students that will not be tolerated under any circumstances. Adopted board policies should include a core policy statement that strongly and emphatically declares that all actions taken by school district officials must be in the best interest of students. A district-level leader pointed out that, "When any individual visits our district's administrative office, the first thing they see as they enter the lobby is a sign which reads: 'IN THE BEST INTEREST OF STUDENTS.'" A superintendent was adamant in noting, "I emphasize over and over to my staff that there is only one reason for our working in this school system — we are here solely to help young people."

It is wise to understand how keeping the importance of making decisions in the best interest of students can help leaders maintain a level playing field in a highly politicized environment. Reminding special interest groups that your job is to do what is best for students can often neutralize opposition.

NOTES:

_____

_____

_____

_____

Corollary 3
An individual should never be employed in the schools unless they love and care for children and youth.

The identification, selection, and employment of school personnel must incorporate effective procedures for determining whether candidates care for the welfare of students. The mistreatment of students, in any manner, must never be tolerated. An elementary principal commented, "I don't care how effective a teacher is in instructing students; if that teacher does not love students, I don't want her working in my school." Another principal pointed out how important it is and how benefits can be reaped when all of the adults who work in a school care about students when she shared, "I have a female custodian in my school who is super at nurturing kids. I consider her to be one of my best employees".

NOTES:

_____

_____

_____

_____

Corollary 4
Unfortunately, there are times when an educational leader has to make decisions where the interests of one segment of the student body might be in conflict with another segment.

Meeting the needs of students with multiple interests is one of the major challenges facing schools. Care must be exercised in assuring that state and federally-mandated accountability programs, which usually focus on minimum standards, do not cause the school to emphasize instruction for one group of students to the detriment of other groups. There is a gray area in which there may not be a best decision. In these situations, leaders must look deeply inside themselves at their beliefs and core values.

NOTES:

_____

_____

_____

_____

ASSESSMENT INSTRUMENT TO DETERMINE THE EXTENT THAT YOU CURRENTLY EMPLOY OR HAVE IMPROVED IN EMPLOYING THE PRINCIPLE OF "WHAT IS BEST FOR STUDENTS" IN MAKING EDUCATIONAL DECISIONS

Instructions: This instrument is designed to help you determine your current status and change in status relative to employing "What Is Best For Students" in making educational decisions. Before reacting to the scale, decide whether you wish to appraise your current practices or the changes you have made in these practices over a particular period of time.

Current Status	*Rating*	*Change In Status*
Uses to <u>very great</u> extent	5	Made <u>significant</u> positive change
Uses to <u>great</u> extent	4	Made <u>some</u> positive change
Uses to <u>moderate</u> extent	3	Made <u>little or no</u> change
Uses to <u>a little</u> extent	2	Made <u>some</u> negative change
Uses to <u>no</u> extent	1	Made <u>significant</u> negative change

Indicators That Decisions and Actions Are Made in the Best Interest of Students	**Rating**
1. Incorporates the "student interest" variable in making educational decisions.	5　4　3　2　1
2. Dramatizes important issues and events to assure positive response.	5　4　3　2　1
3. Strives to develop a school culture that creates support and love for students and education.	5　4　3　2　1
4. Acts in a professional manner by dressing, talking, and behaving like a winner.	5　4　3　2　1
5. Encourages the board to adopt criteria for making decisions in the best interest of students.	5　4　3　2　1
6. Uses visuals, sound bites, etc. that proclaim that the sole purpose of schools is to help students.	5　4　3　2　1

Continued on page 140

7.	Refuses to employ anyone who does not love students.	5	4	3	2	1
8.	Joins colleagues in impressing legislators and other decision-makers that their actions should be consistent with the interest of students.	5	4	3	2	1
9.	Has zero tolerance for the mistreatment of students.	5	4	3	2	1
10.	Protects the interest of students from over-zealous pressure groups.	5	4	3	2	1
11.	Recognizes and celebrates exemplary behavior of employees when they go beyond the call of duty to assist students.	5	4	3	2	1
12.	Sets well-conceived priorities in selecting the most beneficial programs and activities for students.	5	4	3	2	1

ON THE JOB DEVELOPMENT PLANS AND ACTIVITIES
(EMPLOYING THE CRITERION OF WHAT'S BEST
FOR STUDENTS IN MAKING EDUCATIONAL DECISIONS)

Instructions: The purpose of this chart is to provide you with a simple way for you to list your strengths and developmental needs, prioritize your improvement objectives, and list strategies that you might use to reach your goals. Reflect on past experiences and review all personal assessment data, including the previous page, to complete this task.

Strengths	Developmental Needs

Improvement Objectives	Possible Strategies

"BACK HOME" APPLICATIONS
(Employing the Criterion of What's Best for Students in Making Educational Decisions)

Instructions: Based on your understanding of the lesson and the corollaries, pick one or two of the skills and consider your previous experiences and possible future applications "back home" in your leadership role.

SKILL	*PREVIOUS EXPERIENCE*	*FUTURE APPLICATIONS*
The "Bottom-Line" Is Student Welfare, **Dramatization, and** **Employing Personnel Who Empathize With Students**		

SUMMING IT UP AND MOVING FORWARD

Now that you have analyzed the "Twelve Lessons Learned From Experience," I would like you to have the opportunity to review what you have read, summarize your reactions, and decide how you can use these lessons, as well as lessons you have learned from your own experiences. To assist you in accomplishing these tasks, we suggest that you proceed as follows:

1. Reflect on what you have read about the twelve lessons, the accompanying corollaries, and the pearls of wisdom and decide which of these impressed you to the point that you adopt them as your own. Record them on the form labeled – "Lessons I'd Like To Adopt." Some school leaders like to adopt one or more statements for display in their offices or administrative buildings.

2. Following the discussions of each of the "Twelve Lessons Learned From Experience," you were given the opportunity to complete an assessment/behavioral change survey. A summary form has been provided that will allow you to record and analyze the mean (average) ratings from the twelve scales. This summary will provide you with a picture of your relative developmental needs in regard to the twelve lessons.

3. Finally, a form has been provided for you to list your priority developmental needs and some strategies that you might use to address these needs. There is no necessity on your part to limit your developmental needs to the "Twelve Lessons Learned From Experience."

As you complete these tasks and continue working at providing the best education for our country's children and youth, I wish you the very best. I trust you will continue to learn from your and your colleague's experiences – as much as I have learned from compiling and analyzing the experiences of over four hundred educational leaders whom I have enjoyed having in my training programs.

SUMMARY OF RATINGS ASSIGNED TO THE TWELVE ASSESSMENT INSTRUMENTS CONCERNING LEADERSHIP LESSONS LEARNED FROM EXPERIENCE

Assessment Instruments	Items/Your Rating												Mean
1. Competent workers	1	2	3	4	5	6	7	8	9	10	11	12	
2. Valid information	1	2	3	4	5	6	7	8	9	10	11	12	
3. Leader of leaders	1	2	3	4	5	6	7	8	9	10	11	12	
4. Communicating effectively	1	2	3	4	5	6	7	8	9	10	11	12	
5. Opponents of public schools	1	2	3	4	5	6	7	8	9	10	11	12	
6. School boards	1	2	3	4	5	6	7	8	9	10	11	12	
7. Your life	1	2	3	4	5	6	7	8	9	10	11	12	
8. All things	1	2	3	4	5	6	7	8	9	10	11	12	
9. Benefit from mistakes	1	2	3	4	5	6	7	8	9	10	11	12	
10. Networking	1	2	3	4	5	6	7	8	9	10	11	12	
11. Involve others	1	2	3	4	5	6	7	8	9	10	11	12	
12. Welfare of students	1	2	3	4	5	6	7	8	9	10	11	12	

SUMMARY OF YOUR TWELVE ASSESSMENT/BEHAVIORAL CHANGE SURVEY MEAN RATINGS

Instructions: Obtain a mean score or rating for each of the twelve assessment/behavioral change surveys you previously completed and record them in the space provided below. Then rank the means from the highest to the lowest. Items with the lowest ratings or ranks are generally the ones which need additional development.

Lessons Learned From Experience	Mean	Rank
1. Recruits and employs competent workers.		
2. Collects and uses valid information in making decisions.		
3. Strives to be a leader among leaders.		
4. Communicates effectively.		
5. Contends with opponents of public education.		
6. Understands the role and value of the school board.		
7. Keeps work and personal life in perspective.		
8. Accepts that superintendents and schools cannot solve all of society's problems.		
9. Benefits from own critical past experiences.		
10. Employs networking and mentors.		
11. Involves players in analyzing data and developing plans.		
12. Keeps the best interest of students in mind when making decisions and implementing programs.		

LESSONS I'D LIKE TO ADOPT

Instructions: List below the lessons, related corollaries, and pearls of wisdon, which you would like to adopt. Add your own, if you wish. You might want to display your favorites as one-liners in your office or home.

1.
2.
3.
4.
5.
6.
7.
8.
9.
10.

DEVELOPMENT OF PERSONAL AND/OR GROUP IMPROVEMENT PLANS

One of the major purposes of this source book is to provide information and experiences which might assist you with your continuing positive professional development. To accomplish this, you are encouraged to summarize and review your results from responding to the twelve assessment instruments for the Leadership Lessons Learned from Experience and other relevant information about yourself as well. For the purpose of this plan, you will be limited to the following: (1) identifying strengths and developmental needs, (2) setting improvement priorities, (3) formulating objectives, (4) selecting strategies to assure goal attainment, (5) developing an action plan, and (6) designing evaluation procedures.

Identifying Strengths and Developmental Needs

To assist you in identifying your strengths and developmental needs, you are advised of the following:

1. Summarize your results from the twelve assessment instruments concerning Leadership Lessons Learned from Experience which you previously completed. (A form is provided for this purpose at the end of this section.) The mean ratings for the twelve instruments should provide you with a picture of your overall strengths and developmental needs. It follows that the ratings you assigned to each item or statement in the assessment instruments provide you with more specific and detailed information regarding your performance status.

2. After summarizing the results from the twelve assessment instruments, analyze any other personal evaluation information that you may have. Reflect on past experience which will assist you in identifying your strengths and developmental needs. Review all the available assessment information at your disposal and make a list of your strengths and developmental needs

Setting Improvement Priorities

From your compiled list of developmental needs, select the ones which should be addressed to help assure that you will become an even stronger educational leader. You might find it helpful to formulate some criteria for establishing priorities. For example, you might base your decisions on such factors as what your greatest needs are, what you need to improve on to make the biggest impact on students, what change would most please your boss, etc.

Formulating Performance Objectives

After you have determined your priority needs which will be addressed in your personal improvement plan, you need to establish specific performance objectives or goals. When formulating your objectives, you should be guided by the following basic principles:

- Statements of objectives are your commitment to achieve specific measurable end results.

- Your objectives should be consistent with your personal mission, values, and beliefs.

- Your objectives should represent a direct and positive response to identified strengths and developmental needs.

- Objectives should be results-oriented rather than process-oriented.

- Your objectives should be measurable in terms of time, money, quantity, and quality.

Selecting Strategies to Assure Goal Attainment

Keep in mind that strategies are the methods and procedures which you will use to attain your stated objectives. They are stated in brief and rather broad terms. As with the formulation of personal improvement objectives, the wise use of selection criteria could prove to be most helpful in deciding which strategies you will employ to meet your objectives. For example, such factors as cost effectiveness, completion time, and available resources could be employed in selecting the most appropriate strategies.

Developing an Action Plan

To help assure that you implement your strategies efficiently and effectively, you convert your strategies into a workable action plan. Such a plan provides you with a detailed description of the major steps required to meet specific results (objectives) during the implementation of strategies. The action plan is also helpful because it provides you with step-by-step directions, timelines, and personal assignment of responsibilities. The content of the plan is predicated on a progressive, direct cause-and-effect relationship. It also is immediately workable.

Developing an Evaluation Design

To assure that you monitor the progress you make in implementing your personal improvement plan and obtain deserved results (attain objectives), you can develop an evaluation design that is relatively simple and straight forward. At the same time, this design is effective and valid. Such a design could consist of two parts:

- A simple check at the end of each designated planning cycle to determine the extent to which objectives have been obtained.

- The completion of an evaluation form that will measure your effectiveness in implementing the typical strategies and the behavioral changes that you expect to occur as a result of your implementing your strategies.

You might seek the assistance of a researcher or an evaluation specialist to aid you in the development of the evaluation form. The evaluation form usually includes the following:

- A listing of the processes that are involved in implementing your strategies.

- A listing of behavioral changes that you expect to occur from implementing your strategies.

- The development of a rating scale that would allow you and observers to rate your effectiveness in carrying out your strategies and the degree to which you changed your behavior during your improvement initiative.

PRIORITY DEVELOPMENTAL NEEDS

Instructions: On the basis of what you have learned from this book plus additional factors, list several priority developmental needs that are important for you to address in your work. Then, for each need, record possible corrective strategies.

Priority Developmental Needs	Possible Corrective Strategies
1.	1a.
	1b.
	1c.
2.	2a.
	2b.
	2c.
3.	3a.
	3b.
	3c.

USING LESSONS LEARNED FROM EXPERIENCE
TO SOLVE SIMULATED EDUCATIONAL PROBLEMS

One of the safest and most efficient ways to apply the lessons you have learned from experience in solving future educational problems is to read and react to simulated situations presented in the form of case studies. Through this process, you are able to wrestle with dilemmas and enigmas presented in written form rather than experiencing them on the job. Therefore, you will be able to solve "real" problems without the stress and the consequences of failure.

Your participation in this learning activity is quite simple. You begin by reading and analyzing the problem(s) described in one of the following case studies and then try to solve the problem(s) by following the case study analysis guide presented. The analysis process may be undertaken by an individual or a group of people.

CASE STUDY ANALYSIS/DECISION GUIDE

1. Read and analyze the case study.

2. Following your thorough analysis of the case study, decide the following:

   (a) What is(are) the fundamental problem(s) which need to be solved?

   (b) What basic principles, concepts, values, etc. are being compromised or violated in the case study?

   (c) Accepting the fact that you cannot obtain additional information about the case beyond what has been presented to you in written form, what additional data would have helped you in solving the problem(s)?

3. Formulate criteria that you might use in establishing goals and developing strategies to solve the problems identified in the case study. Consider such factors as the impact that your decisions will have on students, costs, policies, politics, preferences of vested interest groups, and the preferences of your boss and peers.

4. On the basis of your analysis of the case study to this point, formulate your objective(s) for improving the situation which has been presented to you. Express your objectives in specific outcome terms.

5. List the strategies that you would employ to meet your stated objectives.

6. Identify the major barriers that you might face in implementing the strategies.

7. In general terms, state how you will evaluate your improvement efforts. Include in your evaluation, statements that will indicate how this exercise has impacted on your knowledge and skills.

8. Take time to review your entire case study improvement plan. Be sure to check to determine whether you have done the following:

   • Addressed the critical issue(s) in the case.

   • Violated school board policy, fundamental concepts, societal values and principles, and the interests of children and youth.

   • Decided that you have a reasonable chance of being successful in implementing your strategies.

9. Make any changes you deem necessary and bring your work to closure.

"ACCOUNTABLE FOR BEING ACCOUNTABLE"

Twelve months ago, you were hired to assume the leadership role in a rural school district which had received high praise and recognition for dramatically improving student performance scores on state administered tests. The superintendent who preceded you had accepted a position as director of testing and accountability with the state education agency. Two years ago he was recognized by his peers for being chosen the state's superintendent of the year. Previous to accepting your current position, you had served as the assistant superintendent in an urban school district which had done very well on the state tests, but not even near the exemplary performance of the school district you now head. You were employed to not only maintain, but to further improve the student test scores in the district. To put it mildly, you consider these expectations to be most challenging and, for the first time in years, you are somewhat apprehensive.

Using your knowledge and skills associated with raising the test scores of students in the district where you had previously been employed, you spent most of the first six months on the job pouring over test results for the past five years and visiting classrooms, especially classes which had a disproportionate number of minority students. From your study and observations, you discovered two things. The test reports issued to the school district showed, without a doubt, that significant gains had been registered for the performance of students on the state tests for the last four years. But your second observation was very confusing. The major strategy that was employed to raise test scores was the use of a diagnostic or prescriptive program which systematically identified and addressed students' weaknesses through the use of a comprehensive pool of test items. From experience, you knew that this approach was sound and, if administered properly, it could bring about significant improvement. To your amazement, however, there was little evidence that the teachers in the schools were using the diagnostic or prescriptive approach effectively. In some classrooms, there was no evidence that the strategy was being employed at all. Furthermore, you were unable to find any consistently viable approaches to improving student test scores in seventy-five percent of the classrooms you observed.

Obviously, you were amazed and wondered what was going on. You asked yourself the following questions: Is there something that I'm missing? Am I losing my ability to observe and recognize quality teaching?

In the morning mail, you received a registered letter that was labeled "confidential" and was signed "anonymous." In short statements, the letter outlined what the writer alleged to be going on with the accountability program in the school district. To your surprise, it revealed both what and who.

Among the major points included in the anonymous letter were the following:

- The assistant superintendent for instruction had formed an accountability committee that was composed of a key teacher and the principal from each of the district's schools.

- The accountability committee had endorsed the diagnostic or prescriptive strategy for improving test scores. Training had been provided to implement the strategy, but participation on the part of principals and teachers was voluntary. The meetings were poorly attended.

- Several months prior to testing, the assistant superintendent for instruction received a registered package from his brother-in-law who was a key staff member of the division of research in the state education agency. The package contained a copy of each test that was to be administered during that year and answers.

- The assistant superintendent made a copy of the test items and the answers for all the tests and distributed these to each teacher on the accountability committee. In turn, the teachers distributed the test items and answers to their peers who began immediately to "teach the test" to their students.

- The only names that were mentioned in the letter were the assistant superintendent, the teachers, and the principals on the accountability committee, as well as the man on the staff of the state education agency.

Upon reading the anonymous letter, you were amazed and apprehensive. You could not envision anyone in education who would join in a conspiracy that had the potential to harm so many people. On the other hand, you knew you faced a dilemma in what you should do with the information you had received. You decided to delay action until the state released the current year's test results to the local school district. You did, however, place a call to the assistant superintendent's brother-in-law in the state education agency and learned that he had left his position six months ago.

Not to your surprise, when the state issued the last test reports to the local school systems, the test scores for your district hit rock bottom! DAMAGE CONTROL!!!

"WHERE THE BUCK STOPS OR GOES"

You have the reputation of being an outstanding school leader especially in selecting and employing strong teachers and support personnel. You believe strongly in defining roles and responsibilities and then allowing your staff to get the job done. The consultants in the state department of public instruction, who enjoy ranking school systems and superintendents, consistently place you among the three top superintendents in the state.

Two years ago, the state board of education obtained funds to conduct a leadership or management study in a number of randomly selected school systems in the state. By draw, you became one of the participants and were interviewed and observed in the early stages of the study. Following the study of you and your school system, the review team issued you an unofficial confidential report so that you could be aware of their findings and begin planning any necessary improvement efforts. The major observations by the study group follow:

- You are very popular and well respected by your school board, the school personnel, and the public.

- Your leadership style is characterized by "let's hire the best, give them the necessary resources to do the job, and give them the freedom to make their own decisions and run the show."

- You depend heavily on two members of your leadership team to help you "run the system." Your deputy keeps you informed about any problems which might be stirring in the schools or community. Your business manager has the responsibility of making sure that no funds are misused and that you always have a substantial balance in your budget at the end of each fiscal year.

- To a great extent, you have an open-door policy. Your personal secretary devotes most of her time to scheduling meetings and conferences for you. Most of your correspondence and necessary clerical work is completed by personnel in the office pool.

- The study committee points out that your major weakness centers around your failure to monitor and hold your staff, especially principals, accountable for their work. They add that this weakness is partially associated with your tendency to rely too heavily on your deputy and director of finance.

- In the final section of your confidential report, the review committee made an interesting comment: "Beware that your strengths might become your weaknesses."

Upon receiving the report from the review committee, you sat down with your deputy and business manager to review your leadership report. Your deputy greatly praised you for the compliments listed in the report. However, he belittled the recommendation concerning your failure to monitor and hold your staff more accountable. Your business manager limited his comments to praise and a statement that we need to continue to emphasize fiscal responsibility. At the conclusion of this conference, you decided not to implement any personal improvement efforts.

Almost one year following your receiving the evaluation from the leadership or management team, your secretary informed you that your business manager wanted to schedule a private meeting with you for an least two hours. The next day, your business manager informed you that approximately two months ago, he observed some suspicious data in the financial report that he was preparing for the school board and you. He noticed that the funds collected and deposited from tickets sold at athletic events at one high school were disproportionately lower than at the other high schools in the district. When checking financial records for the last four years, the same pattern was observed. Your business manager informed you that he did not question the principal or any of the staff at the school with the unusual listings, but it did prompt him to begin a thorough analysis of the current and past financial reports. With a trusted accountant on his staff, the business manager discovered the suspicious entries that follow:

- Three years ago, another high school had deposited significantly fewer dollars from the sale of athletic tickets than other high schools in the district.

- Five schools had made payments to two different vendors for the same equipment and supplies. This had happened over a three-year period. One local vendor was involved in each of the purchase transactions.

- In one school, records indicated that several custodians and cafeteria workers had received payments for services after retiring or leaving their jobs.

- There were dozens of cases throughout the schools where accounting data either indicated sloppy work or a probable misuse of funds.

- Your business manager concluded by informing you that the school district might be facing serious problems related to unethical and illegal use of funds and that what he had observed might be only the "tip of the iceberg."

To put it mildly, you were flabbergasted and alarmed with the business manager's revelations. After regaining a semblance of composure, you said to your business manager, "I want to ask you two questions. Do you think we have a serious problem? And, if so, why haven't you discovered what was going on a long time ago?"

Being a man of few words, the business manager responded in the following way:

> We do have a serious problem, and the reason I did not identify what might have been going on is that I have not kept up with the technology or computer science necessary to do complicated accounting. When we did modernize a few years ago, we didn't purchase the software to identify problems. I simply was not knowledgeable or wise enough to find discrepancies in the financial reports.

You dismissed your business manager with a plea that he keep his findings "under his hat" and for him not to worry. However, you were worried, and yet you realized that to worry was a waste of time. You needed to figure out how to get out of this mess!

"THE BIRDS AND BEES AND MONKEYS THROWING COCONUTS FROM THE TREES"

Pretend that you are a school superintendent in an affluent school district in the Midwest. You have held this position for six years. Except for one problem, your job has been especially easy. Student performance on the state tests has improved each year, and all of your schools have received outstanding ratings. The graduation rate is very high, and a large percentage of the district's graduates enroll in colleges and universities. The problem you face, which has just recently come to the community's attention, is an increasing number of students at the high school and even middle school level who have become pregnant. Despite all of the outstanding accomplishments in your district since you became superintendent, the reputation of the schools appears to be slipping and your ability to lead is being questioned.

The image of the schools and your reputation began declining six months ago when an article appeared in the local paper providing statistics on the increasing number of pregnant students in the schools and a "demand" that the school board and the administration take immediate steps to correct the "deplorable" problem. With the release of the article, the flood gates opened. Over a period of five months, the following events took place:

- Without exception, each week the local paper has carried an editorial elaborating on the problem and demanding corrective action on the part of the schools. In addition, the paper has published numerous letters from readers which both support and condemn the schools, as well as recommend solutions to the problems.

- The superintendent's office has been flooded with e-mails which are mainly very critical of the schools, the school board, and you. In an attempt to bring humor to the flood of mail, the secretaries in your office label the mails as S-E-mail – sex education mail. It was not too long before a pastor in one of the most popular churches in the district wrote a letter to the paper criticizing you for not taking the pregnancy problem seriously.

- At the next monthly school board meeting following the local paper's article concerning the increase in the rate of pregnancies in the schools, five individuals attended requesting to be heard. At the end of the session, the group was recognized at which time they recommended that several local preachers be allowed to provide sex education in the middle schools and high schools. They would emphasize abstinence and the application of religious principles in gender relationships. The school board thanked the visitors for their concerns and informed them that they would schedule a public meeting in the near future at which time people with varying concerns could express their views. This public meeting was scheduled three weeks later.

- Following the meeting, the chairman of the board of education dropped by your office unannounced to discuss the pregnancy issue. During the brief meeting, he advised you to remain in the background and let the board take the lead in trying to solve this problem. He also informed you that, among the five members on the board, two members would probably be liberal in their views while two would be very conservative. Although the chairman did not express his own personal views concerning the issue, you were sure that he would tend to be more liberal than conservative.

- To your surprise, the very next day following your meeting with the board chairman, a front page article in the morning paper revealed that the board chairman and you had met secretly without other board members to plan how to impose your own views and strategies on the citizens in the district in regards to the sex education problem.

- Ten individuals signed up to make presentations at the scheduled public meeting. Four individuals indicated that they represented organizations – the PTA, the local ministerial association, The Lesbian and Gay Support League, and the local youth council in the county. The major points made by the presenters were as follows:

  > Except for one person, the individuals who were not associated with organizations pointed out the seriousness of the problem and requested that the board initiate corrective action. One speaker, however, was adamant in arguing that the schools should not become involved at all in solving the problem. This responsibility should rest solely with the students and their parents.

  > The PTA representative emphasized that the major focus of any corrective action on the part of the schools should be abstinence; but, to protect the best interests of the students, they should be provided with instructions regarding how to protect themselves from disease, emotional trauma, and pregnancy. They recommended that the school should figure out how to distribute condoms in a discrete fashion.

> The representative from the Lesbian and Gay Support League endorsed the distribution of condoms and made a passionate, but surprising recommendation that the school board open and operate a special alternative school for gay middle and high school students.

> The representative from the ministerial association argued that the schools should definitely offer a "family relations" course which would be required for all students. The course would be limited to promoting abstinence and the moral principles associated with family life and sex. The representative suggested that the pastors in the association would be available to teach the course.

> The representative from the youth council, an outstanding senior from one of the high schools, made a plea to the board that middle and high school students be involved in developing and implementing plans to solve the pregnancy problem. He informed all present that the students themselves were most affected by the problem and that they understood the causes and effects better than anyone present at the meeting.

With a few exceptions, the speakers and audience at the meeting were courteous and attentive. One speaker called the members of the school board "a group of jerks," and another ridiculed you for not having any backbone. The representative from the ministerial association was very adamant in saying that students were not mature enough to be involved in solving such a serious problem. A PTA member countered that the involvement of youth was an excellent idea.

Following the close of the meeting, the chairman of the board informed you that this problem was now in your hands. "Come up with a solution!"

A few days later, you learned from a reliable source that school personnel were also beginning to take sides – one group supporting the PTA and the other siding with the ministerial association. Two of your best principals had already assumed leadership roles for the two groups.

"Just what I need," you thought, "more people to muddy the water!"

References

Bennis, W. On Becoming a Leader. Cambridge, MA: Perseus Books Group, 2003.

Bolman, L.G., and Deal, T.E. Leading with Soul. San Francisco, CA: Jossey-Bass, Inc., 2001.

Brubaker, D.L., and Coble, L.D. The Hidden Leader: Leadership Lessons on the Potential Within. Thousand Oaks, CA: Corwin Press, Inc., 2005.

Brubaker, D.L., and Coble, L.D. Staying on Track: An Educational Leader's Guide to Preventing Derailment and Ensuring Personal and Organizational Success. Thousand Oaks, CA: Corwin Press, Inc., 1997.

Drucker, P. Ten Lessons for Leaders. In Leader to Leader. San Francisco, CA: Jossey-Bass, Inc., 1998.

Huff, A.S. Managerial Implications of the Emerging/Paradigm. In Y.S. Lincoln (Ed.), Organizational Theory and Inquiry: The Paradigm Revolution. Beverly Hills, CA: Sage Publications, 1985.

Kaplan, R.E. Beyond Ambition. San Francisco, CA: Jossey-Bass, Inc., 1991.

Kouzes, J.M., and Posner, B.Z. The Leadership Challenge. San Francisco, CA: Jossey-Bass, Inc., 1995.

Posner, B.Z., and Kouzes, J.M. Ten Lessons for Leaders and Leadership Developers, The Journal of Leadership Studies, Vol. 3, No. 3, 1996.

About The Author

Larry D. Coble is Managing Associate of School Leadership Services and Director of the Collegium for the Advancement of Schools, Schooling, and Education at the University of North Carolina at Greensboro. He is co-author of <u>The Hidden Leader: Leadership Lessons on the Potential Within</u> (2005) and <u>Staying on Track</u> (1997) with Dale L. Brubaker.

Coble is former Senior Program Associate at the Center for Creative Leadership. Prior to assuming his current position, Coble served in four superintendencies and during his career has also been a teacher, assistant principal, and principal. A long-time leader of staff development in school districts where he served, Coble has, for the last ten years, worked with numerous leadership development programs, taught at the university level, and served as a private consultant.

For additional information on Lessons Learned, leadership development seminars, and keynote adresses, please contact Larry D. Coble at (336) 315-7710 or (336) 315-7711 or by email at lcoble@schoolleadershipservices.com.

Acknowledgements

One of the training modules most frequently employed training in our work with leaders is a unit called, "Learning From A Master: Yourself." As the topic implies, the training focuses on improving the leadership skills of the participants by getting them to reflect on past experiences and analyze their own strengths and developmental needs, as well as to learn from the experiences of peers, bosses, and those who report to them. Through this process, a wealth of practical leadership lessons have been communicated and recorded. Most of the lessons in this Source Book were a gift from the four hundred or more educational leaders who were involved in training provided by School Leadership Services and who responded to our request for lessons learned on the job. I am indebted to each of those leaders. I hope that this book helps pay that debt.

The whole idea of leadership lessons began for me in the early 1990's when my good friend and colleague, Linton Deck, asked me to join him in working with a group of Louisiana superintendents. Linton was a former superintendent and was at that time director of the education and non-profit applications group at the Center for Creative Leadership. I was a practicing superintendent. We put our heads together and came up with a set of lessons, some of which are indirectly referenced in this work and which later proved to be helpful in analyzing the lessons learned by the practitioners used in this publication. I wish to acknowledge Linton for his contributions to this work.

My longtime friend and writing partner, Dale Brubaker, and I have spent many hours over the years discussing leadership from every possible angle and conceptualizing articles and books. Without question, Dale's influence and insight gained from the work on our previous publications, our current projects, and on-going discussions have helped to contribute to this book. I am grateful for his friendship and wise counsel.

I want to acknowledge the gifted mind of the "Wizard of Wake County" (Raleigh, North Carolina), H. T. Conner, an 83-year-old guru who can still out work most of us who are his juniors. H. T. has worked with me part time since 1985 offering technical support and wise counsel. His fingerprints are on this work.

The senior associate at School Leadership Services is Melody Clodfelter. Melody is the best there is at keeping multiple balls in the air and has helped keep me on course professionally for many years. Prior to her current assignment, she worked with me as a special assistant in my last superintendency. Her "eagle eye" was extremely important in serving as an editor for this project. I wish to thank her and acknowledge her contributions to this project.

Finally, as a teacher at the university level, my courses are filled with students who are working, on a daily basis, in schools and district offices. Their views of lessons learned from experience are to some extent captured in this work. I am grateful for their insights and for stimulating my thinking about how to improve the practice of leadership.

Order Form

You can order <u>Lessons Learned From Experience: A Practical Developmental Source Book For Educational Leaders</u> by calling School Leadership Services at (336) 315-7710, Monday through Friday, 8:00 a.m. through 5:00 p.m., eastern standard time. Orders may also be placed by mail or fax. If possible, please furnish a street address for shipping purposes. Your order will be sent by DHL or US Mail.

Payment may be made by personal check or money order.

Resource	Price	Qty	Total
<u>Lessons Learned From Experience: A Practical Developmental Source Book For Educational Leaders</u>	$29.95	_____	$_____
Please Note: Shipping and Handling Fee: $4.50 per book. The Shipping and Handling cost is for one item shipped within the continental US by US mail or DHL ground service. If two or more items are ordered, the shipping cost will be adjusted, based on the total weight. Overnight delivery is available for additional cost. Quantity discounts are also available.	**Sales Tax 7%** **(NC Only)**		
	Shipping and Handling		
	Total Cost of Order		

ON TRACK PRESS, INC. · **PO BOX 10985** · **GREENSBORO, NC 27404-0985**
PHONE: (336) 315-7710 or (336) 315-7711 · **FAX: (336) 315-7715**
www.schoolleadershipservices.com